BECAUSE YOU CAN

ONE WOMAN'S GUIDE TO LIVING A HAPPY SINGLE LIFE

LISA EDWARDS

RED WOOD TREE

This book contains an extract from *Cheat Play Live* by Lisa Edwards, published by Redwood Tree Publishing in August 2021 on Amazon.

Blog entries first published on the *Because You Can* blog (Wordpress): www.becauseicanblog.com

Cover design: Clare Baggaley

Publisher: Redwood Tree Publishing Ltd

ISBN (ebook): 978-1-7399340-4-0

ISBN (paperback): 978-1-7399340-5-7

Created with Vellum

To Iris, who told me she couldn't decide whether or not she was happier being alone. I hope this helps.

Those who realize the self are always satisfied. Having found the source of joy and fulfillment, they no longer seek happiness from the external world. Happiness can only be found within the self.

BHAGAVAD GITA

INTRODUCTION

I've been writing my blog, *Because You Can* (formerly *Because I Can*), since 2014, about life as a woman of a certain age. I wrote about my experience leaving an unhappy marriage, about being childfree-by-choice, about travelling solo and dating younger men. I wrote about my experiences as a woman 'flying solo' in the world, untethered to someone else, and how it felt 'on the other side' of coupledom. It was a rollercoaster of discovery and I wanted to tell every woman I knew that there was life on the other side, that she didn't have to have a wingperson to hold her hand through life.

I've decided to condense my experience into a handy mini guide that I hope will help others who are thinking about flying solo, either from the position of just having left a partnership, or considering being in one. We are so conditioned to think that the only way through life is hand-in-hand with someone else, so the prospect of living an independent life can be frightening.

When I first left my marriage, I cast around for an 'upgrade' – someone like my husband, only better. Except he wasn't there. The person I was destined to find – and I know it sounds like a cliché – was me. I found, through trial and error, that the greatest freedom was to be found by standing solo in the world; not cutting myself off from others – quite the contrary – but rather not being cut off from them because I was focused on only one other person. For instance, I speak to many more people on solo hikes than I would with a partner by my side.

I hope that you find my seven secrets about single life useful. I've included lots of my blog diary posts so you can witness how I was feeling as I rode the rollercoaster of early solo life, and an extract from my memoir, *CHEAT PLAY LIVE*, which is essentially its full story, from the end of a marriage to full freedom on a Goan beach.

I hope that by reading about my journey, you may realise that coupledom isn't the only path in life – it's just one option. You have a choice. And whatever choice you make, all I ask is that you make that choice with all the information you need.

Because you can.

SECRET 1
YOU DON'T HAVE TO GET MARRIED

THE REALISATION that there were paths other than getting married and 'settling down' came as a surprise to me.

I remember sitting in bar one evening in 2009 with a colleague, Angela, as I was considering leaving my husband. Angela was in her sixties, she wasn't married but she had a boyfriend, whom she didn't call a boyfriend. She lived in her own house in the Peak District and stayed at a friend's flat in London during the week. She had her own life and career and she sparkled with wisdom.

I remember Angela telling me that '*coupledom isn't everything*' and I swear I'd never even considered the idea before she said it. It had seemed to be the ultimate goal of everyone for as long as I'd known, and I wondered whether it was just Angela's own unique path she was referring to – in line with her being a child of the sixties and seventies.

But her words sowed a seed somewhere inside me, and over the years after my marriage, I realised she was right. And now, more than a decade after my eight-year marriage ended, her words still resonate – I wonder why I felt the need to get married at all.

From the age of fourteen, I'd known I never wanted children (see Secret 4) so why would I enter a partnership that is designed to produce them 'legitimately'? Our ancestors only needed marriage to protect bloodlines and provide social and economic stability – love and the concept of a 'life partner' had nothing to do with it at the start.

If you're already socially and economically stable, and you don't want children, why would you bind yourself to one person for life?

Of course, this is a hypothetical question because we all know the reason why we do it. It's consistently presented as the norm by society and the media throughout our lives. It's a constant soundtrack, from fairytales like Cinderella, read as a child, to Disney Princess movies, romcoms and the the royal weddings. They present the fantasy outcome – the perfect union – and many young girls grow up dreaming of their big day. Think of Monica in *Friends* trying on dresses with her friends, and Bridget Jones fantasising about Hugh Grant's groom speech. Those were the TV shows and movies I imbibed before I got married at thirty-five – and inspired by Monica, I was the one who proposed to my boyfriend.

Something inside me propelled me to ask that question even though I knew in my gut that it was wrong on every level. He was the wrong man, I was the wrong woman, and it was the wrong time. I was in a panic to be married by thirty-five – the age that *Sex and the City* told us was 'last chance saloon' – before you were too old to be chosen. In the episode, 'Luck be an Old Lady', Carrie finds herself gambling at the casino in Atlantic City. "What happens after 36?" she asks. "I guess you fall off the table," says the croupier.

I wish I'd known that I had a choice – that I would not only be able to stay on the table, but dance on it too.

ANNIVERSARY
23 NOVEMBER 2014

Today would've been my twelfth wedding anniversary – I got married in 2002 in a small Scottish castle hotel on a crisp, beautiful November day. There were kilts, a ceilidh, fireworks, friends and family. It still ranks as one of the best days of my life, even though the purpose of it has gone away. In many ways, it was a brilliant party that just happened to have a wedding attached to it – I thought so then, and even more so now.

I've often wondered why I felt such a strong urge to get married – I pride myself on not following the usual rules of behaviour – but there I was pursuing this goal because it was just 'what you did'. All my friends had done it or were doing it, and I just had to tick that box. I decided that it had to happen before I was 'too old' to go down the aisle, and that thirty-five was my cut-off point. 2002 was my thirty-fifth year.

I knew it wasn't quite right from the start and yet I pursued it relentlessly. I was the one who asked him to marry me, I was the one who made it all happen, even though he was extremely stressed with work in the year of our marriage and wanted to delay things. I just thought it was procrastination, but in retrospect, maybe he knew it wasn't right either.

We did it anyway, and it was a huge and wonderful party for about seventy of our friends and family. Neither of us had big families, especially as my parents had died and he'd lost his dad, so there were 'missing places' at the wedding that we filled with friends and other loved ones. I made a speech (because of the missing persons) I took myself down the aisle, I arranged the whole thing. I even made myself stay on my own in the hotel the night before, not surrounded by friends and family, and actually a bit scared in the allegedly haunted room. This was all while he enjoyed his last night of freedom with his family and best man back in the village. What was I trying to prove? How alone I could be? I stayed awake pretty much all night.

I knew it was the wrong decision back then, I knew it was wrong on the honeymoon, and I knew for the next eight years. And yet I did it anyway.

I know many people – men and women – who've admitted to me that they've done the same thing and are just going through with it, especially if they have children. It's really scary, even considering leaving a marriage, and it took me time to gain the courage, and crucially, the financial independence to be able to do it.

When I finally did it, it was so sad. By doing what I'd done over the years, and his going along with it, we'd both lived inauthentic lives and it was time to face reality, in our forties. Essentially, we had been great friends who'd lived a great life, filled with adventure holidays, starter homes, dinner parties and burgeoning careers. There was much to be thankful for and the more distance I get on it all, the more I appreciate it for what it was, and him for what he added to my life. Thank you, if by chance you ever read this. (And by the way, I still can't watch *Out of Africa*...)

What I've learned from it all is that your gut instinct is entirely correct, every time, in every circumstance. If your heart isn't in something, your brain and gut know it and they tell you. You must listen to them because they will steer you correctly through life. I've ignored mine in both professional and private life and it's cost me. I suppose this mistake-making is all part of life experience and everyone does this. If only we'd listen to ourselves earlier in our lives and trust in what we hear. That so rarely happens.

I've applied the rule of Gut Instinct to quite a few things now – I only buy clothes if I absolutely LOVE them. Anything less, I know I'll end up going off them and they'll be given to charity. I only accept invitations to things I REALLY want to go to, rather than do things because I think I should, or because 'everyone else' is going. I only maintain friendships with people who truly add something good to my life and at the first sign of toxicity, back away fast, rather than labour away on something worthless.

The downside is that I often trust an initial feeling about something or someone and back away too quickly, making an 'insta-decision' that is so typically too-fast of me. I now catch myself doing it and make myself slow down to really look at the thing or the person, just to see if I'm missing something, if I'm being too hasty. This is the sort of thing I do when I visit new countries – I go there with all my preconceptions and first impressions and then wait for the reality to reveal itself.

It's fun, waiting to be disproved about something,

because you know, your gut instinct is usually telling you there's something in there worth waiting for.

SECRET 2
YOU DON'T NEED A WINGPERSON

Once I'd left my marriage at forty-three, I did two things: I waited for another partner to step out of the shadows to claim his prize (me) and when he didn't appear, I cast about for a husband upgrade. He didn't appear either. It came as a huge shock to me, that a fit, healthy, smart, attractive woman with her own economic stability (I was a high-flying publishing director) and no urge to have children would not be a desirable candidate as a partner – especially not for a man the same age as her.

Now I know that it is a truth universally acknowledged that a single middle-aged man in possession of a fortune must be in want of a (no older than thirty-five) wife, but for some reason I'd forgotten what Carrie Bradshaw told me and I found myself on the floor, having fallen firmly off the dating table.

I cast about wondering what to do next, no longer validated in society by being positioned next to a life partner. I wondered where my tribe were: I couldn't hang out at the school gates with women my age because I'd chosen to be childfree. For a while I was caught in a limbo, unable to join the couples' dinner-party brigade, but seemingly too old to join the singles' houseparty scene too.

But slowly, I realised that I was placing limits on myself because of the things that society had taught me were 'normal'. I began to explore friendships with younger people and a social scene in the area I'd moved to in West London from my marital home in Buckinghamshire. I began to join hiking groups where I met independent women in their thirties and forties like me, unable to find suitable men their own age, and told them what I'd learned post-marriage. I met younger men who were only too happy to date me – and they made me feel alive again.

I also found that I wanted to celebrate my independence by going out more and making up for all the party time I'd lost as both a married woman and a Catholic girl who had been 'good' all her life. I made friends with women who'd already sown their seeds and wanted to go home to bed. So I started socialising with myself, taking myself out to bars, restaurants, clubs and even gigs. I found a world beyond the school gates and marital homes and for me, there was no looking back.

THE ONE WHERE I'M ABSOLUTELY NOT A YUMMY MUMMY

17 AUGUST 2014

LAST NIGHT, getting off the London Overground at Kensal Rise, I was accused by a group of drunk, loud-mouthed, relatively posh boys of being a 'yummy mummy'.

I had heard them shout, "Welcome to middle England!" as the train pulled into the station and had scowled in their general direction. This prompted them to follow me on the platform, saying, "I bet she's married to an advertising executive!" (wtf?) and then shouted, "She's a yummy mummy, wearing jogging bottoms!"

It took all my strength not to turn round, face them on a full platform, to say, "Actually, I'm a single, childfree, publishing executive who eats boys like you for breakfast."

In reality, I was on my way back from a day-long hike, wearing leggings and cross-trainers. The boys had confused me with the mums' yoga tribe that is part of the rich fabric of the Kensal Rise and Queen's Park community. They're everywhere – usually in their late thirties or forties, skinny, wearing drapey jersey items, holding a juice or a green tea from a local cafe and either looking zenned-out from yoga or looking a bit fraught. The only bit of that list I tick is the age one, and maybe the odd drapey jersey item. And yeah, ok, I was looking a bit frazzled after the hike.

The YM is the predominant fortysomething female tribe in my area and I'm not part of it. I moved here two years ago after my separation, and thought a lot about how to infiltrate its ranks, wanting to make new friendships with women of my own age. I joined a local group that has events for women but the tribal subsets were already set in stone. You see I'm not at the school gates, in the morning yoga class or at the coffee meet-up at our local deli so to them, I'm pretty much invisible.

After a while I stopped trying to infiltrate. In the main, the friendships I've forged here are with younger people. I'm lucky enough to be surrounded by a great set of people in my building – the infamous 'gold building' in Kensal Rise – and we socialise a lot. I set up a Facebook page for residents to facilitate it and I've met some really wonderful, genuine people.

At first I was acutely conscious of the age gap – they're anything from late twenties to late thirties – and kept pointing it out every time we went to the pub. There were genuine looks of puzzlement: "What are you on about?!" they'd say. But there is a societal stigma about middle-aged people who hang out with younger ones, like they've never matured enough to keep up with their peer group or they're trying to hard to hang on to their youth.

But what if you've done the whole mature couply thing for quite a long time, decided it wasn't for you, re-entered non-couply society and found that most of the people at your age are still at the mature couply party? It is one party I'm happy not to be attending right now, but I've had to accept that I've left the cosy weekend dinners for six round at someone's house, planned weeks or months in advance, for spontaneous meet-ups at the pub with whomever happens to be around, followed by dancing at Paradise or a party back at someone's flat.

Long live spontaneity, in my view.

Because my new local friends have welcomed me into their lives as a person they want to hang out with, I no longer feel the urge to refer to myself as 'the oldie' – it just seems inappropriate now. What's particularly lovely is that I have a couple of young couples in my circle of friends whom I love dearly. Back when I was in coupledom, we'd never have thought about hanging out with a single friend, so strong was the tribal urge to bond with other couples, and the stigma around their situation. Thank goodness that little 'rule' has been broken.

One thing I've grown to loathe in life is the way some people try to box you up, in a category that is age-appropriate. I cringe when I hear people say, "But he's eighteen, so of course he's just going to want to hang out with his mates, get drunk, have lots of sex and go wild at music festivals." What if he's eighteen, wants to concentrate hard on his studying, hang out in a coffee shop on his own, have a little bit of sex, or no sex, and camp with one good friend in a remote village in Wales? Why do we pressure people to tick all the age-related boxes?

Similarly, one might hear someone say, "But she's thirty-five, she's going to want to find a man quickly, marry him, have a child, buy a house and enjoy weekends at B&Q."

Aaagh! What if she wants to take a gap year to travel, concentrate on her career, date several men without marrying them, and rent in a really cool place that doesn't require DIY? You can see where I'm going with this.

People assume stuff about me. I know they do. They see me on a train, running in Queen's Park or walking down the road to Portobello and think, "Married, just been to yoga class while the kids are at school, off to have lunch at an artisanal cafe that sells vintage furniture on the side, before picking up Tarquin and Oberon from school and making them eat quinoa for supper."

Sometimes I feel like wearing a '*Baby On Board*'-style badge that says: '*Single, childfree, not doing what you think I'm doing.*'

I assume stuff about people too – I wish I didn't. I assumed younger people wouldn't be interested in getting to know me, I assumed other fortysomething women would want to welcome me into their tribe even though I wasn't wearing the right headdress, I've assumed fortysomething men would want to date me.

Wrong, wrong and wrong.

But there is something so right, right, right about not being in a tribe. Or building one of your own.

Because you can.

A BAR OF ONE'S OWN

12 DECEMBER 2014

One of the main topics on my 'must blog about' list for Because I Can has been the concept of drinking alone. Not just sitting on my sofa watching TV with a nice chilled Prosecco or Picpoul De Pinet in the fridge – actual Going Out To A Bar On My Own.

I've been doing it for around four years now, on and off, so it's become part of normal life for me, but it still amazes some people when I mention it and I find myself explaining what I do, how I do it, and reliving all those moments in bars that happened on my way to normalising this activity for myself.

It all began back in the Camino bar near King's Cross. I'd already separated from my husband and was hitting the after-work social scene quite hard. On the odd occasion, all of my friends were busy doing other things and I became frustrated that my social life depended on other people being available. Why did it have to be like that, I thought? If I want to go out, I should be able to go out, just as guys do, with a newspaper and a pint at the end of the bar. But as we all know, if a woman does that, an assumption is made that she is touting for business, and I don't mean hoping a recruitment consultant will buy her a drink.

I became determined to try it out so one night I took a copy of the *Evening Standard* to Camino – a very busy after-work bar filled with 'young professionals'. I was maybe pushing the age range up a bit just by walking in. I went to the bar, ordered a glass of wine, took a perch on a bar stool and studied my newspaper.

Nothing happened. No one stared, no one propositioned me, no one cared. It felt amazingly liberating. So I did it again.

I found that sitting on a bar stool right next to the bar offered me the most 'invisibility'. People assumed I was just waiting for someone, or at least just there temporarily. I took work with me, or read a book, and barely looked up at the people around me – it was just so easy to blend in. I enjoyed the look on guys' faces as they saw me finish my drink and leave the bar. "Oh my god, she was actually on her own, not waiting for someone!" Ha.

Every now and again someone would notice me. Usually a woman. In a pub in Belsize Park one stood next to me at the bar and asked, "Are you here, alone?" Yes, I replied. She told me how much she admired me for it and promptly ordered me a glass of wine. I watched her go back to sit with her partner and they both looked at me admiringly as I grinned back. I loved it.

I haven't always been looked at admiringly by women for doing this. I noticed that if I went to bars alone on holiday, as I did in Thailand on my first solo jaunt, I'd see a (usually British) couple in a corner, the woman glowering at me and the man looking impressed. I don't know why these women felt annoyed by me being on my own but I have experienced it a few times.

Only this year in Turkey, an older British woman, with her more-impressed husband, told me she thought people who holidayed alone were "sad" and she "felt sorry for them." As I left them sitting smugly on the beach to go shopping, I thought, "I'd rather be heading to a bar in Bodrum on my own than sitting next to you on a beach, love."

Now it's just part of my normal routine to take myself off to a pub now and again. After a hard day of meetings, I like nothing better than grabbing a copy of *Grazia* and ordering myself a glass of wine in my local pub. The bar staff know me and every now and again someone I know joins me. If they don't, no biggie. I don't need a wingperson. I know lots of people who can't go anywhere without one – going running, to a bar, shopping, on holiday – all of these things I do on my own. It's uniquely liberating. Why wait for someone else to validate your activities when you can own them yourself?

Whilst going to a bar alone might shock some people, what about going to a club? I've done it, lots of times. In a busy environment like a club, no one knows you're on your own. You may have become separated from your friends, you may have just arrived and are looking for them. No one notices. It's easy to slip in, grab a drink, go for a dance and slip out again. Oh the joy.

I started doing it because my friends tended to end nights out earlier than I wanted to end them. We'd go out for a drink or a meal, and I'd be back in my flat at 9.30pm/10pm itching to carry the night on. I got so frustrated by it one night that I just thought, 'fuck it' – I'm doing it. What would a guy do? He'd just go out and see who was there. So I did.

About half the time I've done it, I've bumped into people I know. When I haven't, I've survived it. Loved it, even. People are so caught up in their own bubbles that no one notices me: at the bar, on the dance floor, moving between rooms. I'm just a woman in a club, albeit older than the average. Do I care about that? No. And seemingly no one else does.

I haven't done my club routine in a while because once I'd done it a few times I'd largely got it out of my system. It's no longer a case of me feeling like I'm missing out on something when the evening ends 'early', it's more that I know what's out there should I want to take it further, and I can if I want to. The night is never over if I don't want it to be and it's not forbidden territory – it's there for the taking if I want it.

Because I can.

SO LONELY

10 JANUARY 2016

I'VE JUST FINISHED WATCHING the BBC's *The Age of Loneliness* on iPlayer – it's a really poignant documentary featuring interviews with a range of people of all ages from 19 to 90, who are prepared to admit that they are lonely.

I sat there listening to the stories of 70- and 90-year-olds still yearning for the company of their spouses – one keeps his wife's ashes in a bag on the chair next to him – and thinking about my own mother's story. Her husband died when she was my age, and her life pretty much folded. By choice.

Her friends reached out to her, tried to involve her in social events, but she removed herself from them. She went so far as to move us all to a little bungalow on a hill above the town and kept herself to herself for another twenty years. This is not, as you may have guessed, going to be a template for my next twenty years...

What struck me about the programme was how many people were conditioned to only consider a life alongside a wingperson. The thought of living without a 'significant other' was leading some of them to suicidal thoughts. They admitted to not liking their own company and not being able to even think of a future without a 'pal' (but by 'pal' they meant a relationship partner).

I've gone there. I've thought about that. I've been thinking it for a while and the words 'my romantic life is over' have been going around in my head for a few years. At first, in a horrifying way, and more recently in a much more accepting way. And it's ok. I don't need a wingman (or a wingwoman for that matter). It's quite a liberating moment in your life.

Last year I listened to the incredible Kim Cattrall talking in a positive way about her romantic life being 'retired' and almost cheered as she went on to tell *BBC Woman's Hour* how this wasn't a negative thing, and about all the people and things she had going on in her life. I'd already been working my way towards that position myself, but here was a woman, admittedly a decade older than me, but describing my current views on how to live life.

Contrasting with that, *BBC Woman's Hour* broadcast a new-year programme, in which a lovely woman called Edwina phoned in and talked about the loneliness she felt after losing her husband. She burst into tears during the call and cried out the words, "I lost my husband!" and all of us listeners' hearts broke for her. I was on the Overground with tears in my eyes.

But my next thought was less sympathetic. I found myself thinking it was a shame that Edwina had only lived life as her husband's Siamese twin and had expected that to go on *ad infinitum*. There appears to be a generation of women that can't cope when their husbands leave them or die before them (and statistically women outlive men). My mother was one of them.

Last night I went to see *The Danish Girl* alone. I'd been

shopping all day, had my hair done, then took myself for a quick prosecco in a central London bar before realising I was due at the cinema within the hour. I posted on Facebook about the movie and immediately women of my age were responding saying they'd love to go, but they couldn't find anyone to go with them. Going solo is now so normalised for me, I still find it surprising when people are so worried about doing it.

Consider this. It's never a case that people are staring at you when you're doing things on your own, thinking you're weird – it's you, staring at yourself thinking you're weird. Once you stop looking at yourself in that way, the demons will take flight and you'll be standing there laughing, wondering how you could've been so daft about it. People will talk to you, smile at you, admire you, even buy you a drink.

If you can get you to smile at yourself, admire yourself and buy yourself a drink, even better. I'm a Kim, not an Edwina. And I'm not moving to a remote hilltop to live like a hermit any time soon.

SECRET 3

YOU CAN DATE WHOMEVER YOU WANT (AND IT DOESN'T HAVE TO BE FOREVER)

One of the joys of being a newly single woman in her forties (and even if you're not single) is realising that younger men are interested in you. I first realised it at a work party at the age of thirty-eight and asked the guy in question if he was checking me out. "Yes!" he cried sheepishly, astonished that I'd put it into words.

Once I'd spotted his attention, I started spotting it everywhere – a cheeky glance here, a sexy grin there. It was a thing and I couldn't unsee it. I'd got so used the narrative of men my age dating younger women that it never occurred to me that it could also work the same way for women of my age. Following a few false starts with men my own age, so began a decade of dating younger men which has continued to this day.

One night, in November 2013, I went to a networking event where tech entrepreneur, Cindy Gallop, was speaking on a panel about women in business. Her opening line was, "I'm fifty-three and I date younger men." I was immediately enthralled. She was in control of her life – her career, her relationships – in a way I'd never heard a woman speak of before. Like me, she was childfree-by-choice and husband-free-by-choice. In an interview on the Huffington Post blog in 2016 she said:

"I realized relatively early on that I had no desire to be a mother whatsoever. I actually love children, but specifically other people's. I have three nieces, three nephews, four god-daughters, and a godson, all of whom I adore, and that does me just fine. And I've never felt any particular desire to be married. There was no active, conscious decision-making point, just a gradual realization over time that I'm very happy minus children and marriage."

Cindy had what she called "*casual and recreational*" relationships with younger men, and to my knowledge, still does. I found her approach to life revolutionary and so in line with my own experience. I had the same criteria for selecting men, which I did on the burgeoning dating-app scene at the time:

"No matter how casual the relationship, I have one fundamental criterion: they have to be a very, very nice person. I have excellent radar for very, very nice people, and as a result I only date utterly lovely younger men, in a context of mutual trust, respect, affection, and liking. A number of these casual relationships last a great deal longer than other folks' committed ones..."

I found I could easily find the nice young men who were keen to date me, and I did, with relationships lasting from two months to two years. I found that people would question why I invested in something that apparently couldn't be long-term, and found myself asking, "Why does it need to be long-term?" Why are we conditioned to think we have to be with the same person forever and ever, amen?

Over the years, I grew to realise that I am someone who seizes the day rather than waits for the future. So many years can be wasted waiting for 'the one' and I'm grateful that I realised this in time to enjoy 'the ones'.

SIXTH DATE SYNDROME

19 SEPTEMBER 2014

One of the things I did in the first couple of years after my marriage broke up was date men my age, looking to see if there was a potential new partner out there for me. One would assume that there might be, no?

I sallied forth and met some really great fortysomethings, either online dating, through friends or via social media. But what I didn't know when I started dating them was that each and every one of them would run away screaming after the sixth date.

I met 'Simon' through two mutual friends in a pub. Quiet, dryly funny, smart and a bit of a silver fox. I thought I'd take the initiative (I usually have to) and ask him if he'd like to go out. I gave him a business card and I think he texted me at some point and we started dating.

We did the usual fortysomething thing of nice bars, good wine, lovely restaurants. We chatted about travel, our jobs, previous relationships and I really enjoyed his company. He seemed 'sorted' – a good guy.

One weekend, after the sixth great date, I was in my

kitchen making coffee, while he was sitting in another room. I thought I'd suggest we go for a walk 'sometime' on Hampstead Heath. I heard an audible groan.

I stuck my head round the door and shouted, "Hey – don't sound TOO excited!" expecting him to say, "Sorry, I just stubbed my toe on your coffee table", but what I got was complete silence.

Tumbleweed.

Then later that week, when I texted him to ask what was going on, I got two huge 'text essays' explaining (mansplaining) that I was clearly "looking for something serious" and he wasn't.

"Unbelievable," I texted back. It was like an episode out of *Sex and the City*, but minus the Post-It Notes.

[*I later found out he'd gone back to his ex*]

I met 'Daniel' through social media. A louder version of Simon and an uber 'foodie'. We had six really great dates featuring great restaurants, cocktail bars and movies. On the sixth date, I decided to tell him I liked him. Just that. "I like you," with a winning smile.

Not, "I'd like to marry you", or "I'd like to have your babies" or "I'd like to share your financial gains". Just, "I like you."

I didn't hear from him for two weeks, after which point I started getting 'nighttime' texts from him, trying to recalibrate the dating back to a more 'casual' setting. He'd told me before that he enjoyed dating because it meant he got to try new bars and restaurants. I think I was just the 'caddy' to the foodie.

Nah. Think I'll leave it there, thanks.

So when I met 'Paul' I thought I'd test my theory again. Three strikes and I'm out.

Paul had recently split from his wife, which was bound to be tricky, but we got on incredibly well, especially intellectually. Funny, smart, worked in media – lots to talk and laugh about. Until I told him I liked him on the sixth date.

I've never seen anyone row away so fast. And again, the ensuing text essay 'mansplaining' how he couldn't commit to anything. I wasn't asking him to. Sigh.

I would lay money on that scenario happening again, but I haven't dated any fortysomethings for a while so haven't had a chance to test my theory again recently. They're not a demographic that are particularly interested in me and I've blogged before about them wanting younger women so that they can a) fuel their midlife ego and b) possibly have children.

Well, having encountered Sixth Date Syndrome I'm not particularly keen on them either and really, I'm too busy fuelling my own midlife ego crisis.

What really irks me is the assumption that I want something out of them, that I'm trying to lay a commitment trap of some kind. That just by saying I like them, they translate it as, "...and I want to marry you and have your babies."

Way to think too much of yourselves, guys.

I've done the commitment thing and come out the other side. I'm very clear about not wanting children, and really, way past that childbearing age. What if I actually do like hanging out with you and want to do it on a regular basis without raiding your bank account? Ooh, SCARY.

Am I really that intimidating, with my good job, own flat, ability to hold a conversation, tell a joke and initiate sex? Apparently so.

Anyway, fortysomething men, see you when we're all in our sixties and still out there. At least we will be able to share our stories of how much fun it was to date younger men and women, eh?

Looking forward to it.

IN PRAISE OF YOUNGER MEN

23 AUGUST 2014

I DATE YOUNGER MEN. Or rather, they date me. All of that 'cougar' predatory-female stuff is just nonsense – they're the ones on the prowl. They sometimes try to laugh it off by saying that I'm 'on the hunt' but I'm not. They are. And more often than not, they've made the first move.

When I was 38, I started to notice that my 'attention demographic' had shifted. I'd never really attracted the attention of twentysomethings when I actually was one, but suddenly I started noticing a glance here and there, a cheeky grin or even a wink.

At first I thought I was imagining things but I 'checked in' with one guy who was at a party I was at, clearly giving me the eye and he confirmed it. He was interested.

At that time I was still married so nothing happened but I started to notice furtive glances all over the place. By the time I was set free I was keen to test the water, so to speak. And oh, the joy.

Once you've weeded out the PUAs [*pick-up artists*] and the ones just ticking a box on their life to-do list, there are some really lovely guys out there who just like dating older women.

I'm going to change the names of the guys involved, but here are the moments that have been some of the happiest times in my life, brought to me by this unexpected target audience.

The Spontaneous One

Liam met me in person for the first time at a Muse gig in Wembley Stadium (social media is telling me this was four years ago this week). It could have gone horribly wrong: we'd met online and I found myself offering him my spare ticket (not a euphemism). I spotted him outside the venue, looking a bit uncomfortable. By the time we'd had a beer, and I'd convinced him to remove his shades, we were getting on really well. Luckily.

An older couple were sitting next to us in the stands and Liam told me later that after we'd kissed, he'd turned round and found the woman scowling at him and the guy giving him a thumbs-up and a wink. Brilliant.

The Risk-Taking One

Niall was an apprentice engineer and lived at home with his god-fearing family. Under the guise of doing 'overtime' at work he came to meet me, on his motorbike. He was beautiful, and a really bright, emotionally mature young man. He boasted to all his friends that he was seeing an 'actually hot 43-year-old.'

How we laughed.

Particularly on those occasions when he avoided church and worshipped me instead. Ha.

The Thoughtful One

There are actually a few of these – guys who bothered to arrange days or nights out and put in the effort.

There was Harry, who bought a load of ingredients round to my flat after work and made me dinner, followed by a day out at a stately home.

Back then, I was worried what people would think, seeing me hand-in-hand with a gorgeous tall, blond twentysomething, but he insisted. No one even blinked an eye and it was one of those magical days.

Then there was Zayn, whom I always arranged to meet in a pub. He always texted beforehand to tell me exactly where he was sitting so I wouldn't have an awkward moment in the bar, and when I got there, he'd have bottle of wine and two glasses, ready to go.

One night, while Zayn was at the bar, I overheard a woman in the pub bemoaning her relationship woes to her male friend. She pointed at me and said, "I want to do what she's doing." As my date returned to the table I beamed with pride.

And then there was Louis. Half-Irish, half-Jamaican, about six foot five. Last summer he took me to Regent's Park and when I met him, he'd bought champagne, strawberries and lots of other good things. I laughed as we strolled through the park to find a picnic spot and everyone – male and female – gawped at his beauty.

He once drove past me unexpectedly, shouted my name, stopped the car, ran across the road to tell me I looked gorgeous, ran back to his car and drove off. What a guy.

The One That Asks You Out Properly

I can count the number of times I've actually been asked out from a cold, standing start, on one hand. Less than one hand, in fact.

And the ones that have asked me out on a date, properly, are younger men who aren't British. Go figure. The sweetest one asked if he could take me out for a cup of tea. Just lovely. Of course I said yes.

The One That Slightly Breaks Your Heart

Of course, one of the sidebar themes of dating younger men is that it can never be a 'thing'. It's very much 'dating in the moment' and there is usually an unspoken, or spoken, agreement at the start that it won't lead to a relationship. There is both joy and sadness in being together, and with one particular guy, let's call him Justin, we even cried a little at the start because we knew we had strong feelings for each other.

Against my usual rules, I let myself become more than just a lover with Justin. One of the things that is so intoxicating about a younger man is their engagement with life. Everything is exciting and new, even a fortysomething woman. I loved how Justin lived his life – he worked hard, played hard, and wanted to know and experience everything. To me, it was an elixir of life I couldn't stop imbibing.

This situation could not be sustained and after a couple of months it became clear that it wasn't going to work. I was thrown for a while into a mini mid-life crisis. I realised that I was so jealous of Justin's youth – that he could simply find someone else straight away (he did) and carry on opening all of life's doors. I had to cut off all social-media contact so that I couldn't witness it – it suddenly seemed like a relentless stream of The Joy of Youth and I had to turn it off at the source.

But as the months went by, I found myself looking back on that time with increasing gladness. Dr Seuss' maxim: *"Don't cry because it's over, smile because it happened"* became my way of describing the feeling.

I'm still smiling.

The Years

Some friends say to me that it's all very well having fun with these young guys, but when am I going to get serious and find someone my own age, or older? Guys my age aren't interested, I reply. They want someone younger, especially if their dream is to have kids (and it usually is). (They're also often threatened by someone successful with a brain, but that's for another post.)

That's been one of the really unexpected twists in my post-marital world. I thought there might be guys my age who would pop out of the woodwork. Instead, I was met by a vast silence, punctuated with approaches from married men (I'm afraid so), and the stealthy advance of the younger guard. And I say again, it's their advance, not mine.

For months, and maybe a couple of years post-divorce, I found myself trying to recreate the same-age coupledom that I'd had with my ex-husband. It was 'almost' irritating to have young men buzzing around me, with the promise of nothing long-term. Almost.

But as time has gone on I've realised something: what if these are The Years? The ones where I have the most fun with the beautiful young men that I didn't date when I was their age? What if these moments of joy with these great guys are the things I will whisper about happily when I'm on my deathbed?

I am definitely a late-bloomer – I look and feel so much better than I did in my late teens and twenties and back then, I led a very sheltered, Catholic-upbringing, worried-about-everything, date-free existence. Is this the time I make up for all that?

Well, yes I think it is.

Because I can.

THE LOVE LANDSCAPE

10 SEPTEMBER 2017

I've been wondering for a while now, about how to encapsulate the particular state a late forty- or fiftysomething single woman finds herself in with regards to relationships. Every time I go on a group hike, there is the inevitable conversation with a woman around my age, who is confident, intelligent, attractive, adventurous – I'd even go as far as to say 'sparkling' – and before we've even discovered each other's names I know what she's going to say.

She's going to tell me that she's tried dating men her own age (the rare ones that don't want to date younger women), but they can't quite keep up with her in terms of get-up-and-go or sex drive. They don't want to get out and do things as much as she does and she ends up leaving them behind to join hiking groups at weekends.

She's going to say that she has her eye on someone a bit older, but then discovers that they're dating someone twenty years younger than them, because they can. She's going to say that she gets quite a lot of interest from younger men, but she wants someone to share a present and a future with and they don't offer much in that way, because they're just after the 'mature' experience. And they're largely immature.

Then she's going to share a recent experience where she's been chatting to a guy her age online and it's been going really well, but then he mysteriously disappears, reappears, then disappears again. In search of answers, she'll tell me that men have called her 'scary' or 'out of their league' and I'll nod in agreement. I too am a scary woman.

We then walk along together, chuckling in solidarity as we watch the guys our age and older chatting up the young women, sometimes the hike leader, and the young men chatting with anyone but us (for more than a few minutes). Interest from them comes in secret, by private message, maybe after the hike – but it can never happen in broad daylight. They can't be seen to be into us. The horror!

Not that hiking is about finding people to date, but that is an inevitable sidebar of a group that is mixed and into the same things. (I laughed yesterday when one thirty- or fortysomething guy was talking about not wanting to be part of outdoor groups where fifty- or sixtysomethings hung out. I didn't bother telling him my age.)

I recently went to an event where a late-forties guy friend turned up with his girlfriend of twenty-seven. Another older guy friend discovered the news and had that look on his face when he reported back to our group – the one I've seen before when the same topic comes up among men. The "I didn't realise we could do that" face. You can almost hear their brains working out how they could trade in their old model for a new one. I remember one of my ex-husband's friends starting to date a girl in her twenties when he was nearly forty and it was like he'd scored a try for Scotland when his friends found out. I didn't realise back then what a 'coup' it was. I also didn't realise back then that I could play those guys at their own game.

Older men say to me that they want to date younger women because they still want children, but I don't believe that to be true. I believe that they don't want to date someone who is their equal in terms of 'social power' so they look for someone who is below their perceived standing. I've made my peace with that. I don't want to date someone who is scared by my social power either. It's really unattractive.

I seem to have recently acquired a crop of younger guys who can only message me when they're drunk or high. Some are in relationships, some not, some are struggling to come to terms with being attracted to an older woman. In it comes, the text or WhatsApp message in the morning, sent at 2am. Sometimes they've been up all night and I get the '*hey babe*' at 10am. We never meet up, and nothing ever happens.

For some reason the message frequency ramps up around early spring and autumn – I'm told it's something to do with testosterone levels. I quite enjoy seeing what the morning brings when I switch my phone on, and I can't seem to bring myself to block their numbers either. There's a fascinating increase in messaging when I'm on holiday. Suddenly when I'm thousands of miles away on my own, I'm incredibly attractive. The minute I arrive home the silence descends. It's a thing.

One guy who has appeared and disappeared from my life for over a decade, always seems to get in touch when I'm on holiday. We're not connected on social media, but he seems to have a sixth sense for when I'm away. He's suddenly telling me that he thinks he fucked up by letting me get away, that there might be a relationship there. He is four years younger than me but obsessed with the age gap.

Like every younger man, he wants to know the age of the youngest guy I've ever slept with. I still don't know why that matters (give me wine and I'll tell you the number).

What was fascinating, before his predictable disappearance on my return, was his reaction to my saying that I have a lover. He kept coming back to the topic over and over, but not saying the word. He referred to my 'friend', my 'boyfriend', my 'fuck buddy', my 'friend with benefits' and over and over I corrected him. "He's my 'lover'", I said. Why could he not comprehend it or type the words? Was it because it sounded a bit '60s or '70s?

'Lover' accurately describes the state of being with someone you care for deeply – not in an official relationship, not seeing them every day or even every week, but they are in your life and you acknowledge and love their space in it. My lover is thirty-two and Muslim and we know it can never be a thing, but I'd rather be with him – a man who is straightforward, kind, sexy and not scared of me in the slightest – than with a man whose idea of flirting is relentless 'teasing' (aka bantz).

Perhaps what I'm doing – maintaining my adventurous independence but with a love interest on the side – is a female version of the 'I didn't realise we could do that' face. As more and more women my age opt out of marriage and into independent lover-dom, I feel like we're the ones scoring the tries. The more I talk about it with other women, the more I think that we're scary to more conventional men because we've discovered the big secret – we have a choice, and it doesn't need to include them. Sure, it would be nice if it did, but if it doesn't, our worlds don't end.

In fact, they open up.

SECRET 4
YOU DON'T HAVE TO HAVE CHILDREN

Although I knew in my gut at the age of fourteen that I never wanted children, I found the pressure from society to have them as I got older very hard to push back against. Just like marriage, it's there, in the ether, told in stories in every conceivable (pun-intended) way. If I so much as smiled at a baby in my thirties – and contrary to popular opinion, I do – someone would say, "Ooh look! Lisa's broody!" I wasn't – I just liked that particular tiny human being.

I know that this chapter won't be for everyone, but I'm putting it here for those that might not realise that they have a choice, that having children is optional. Yes, it's a natural function of the body but you don't have to use your body to do it. Mine has never done it and it is not complaining. When anyone asked why I wasn't partaking, I would always answer, "I'm not here to do that." I've always known, on a cellular level, that it's not my role here on Earth.

I'm in my fifties now and I've never for a single moment regretted that decision. My ex-husband has gone on to have children with his new partner and I'm happy for him. I'm also happy that for myself, outside of a pandemic, I have no ties or responsibilities to anyone and I can travel and work wherever I like. I don't need to do the school pick-up, go on holiday at set times or hang out in play parks filled with screaming. This is what freedom looks like to me.

Some people say that they have children so they might have someone to look after them when they're old. Experience has shown me that this is not necessarily true but the truth about having children is shrouded in mystery (some might say necessarily, or we'd never do it).

A number of friends have whispered privately to me about the daily drudgery of it, especially in the early months and years. I don't know how I already knew it was such hard, relentless work, but I did. I would never make such a huge, life-changing decision without knowing the full facts about what I was letting myself in for so I'm hoping this book helps someone out there to at least ask some questions before they take the plunge.

If you're wavering over the decision, talk to a good friend who's gone there. Find someone whom you know will tell you the truth about their experience and only then make an informed decision. Just know that you have a choice, and that choice is a wonderful, freeing thing.

Make sure you avoid the Baby Mafia – people who are intent on getting you to join 'the gang' because they need their decision to be validated. A mum friend told me about them early on so I could see them coming (she also told me she felt she'd lost her identity to her children). Beware – the Baby Mafia are sometimes men, as I know from being harassed at a friend's wedding about my childfree status. This particular man couldn't let the subject go – questioning me endlessly about my choice at the wedding breakfast. In the end, my ex-husband had to ask him to lay off. He was a keen traveller and my sense was that he hadn't bargained on losing so much of his freedom. He was annoyed that I still had mine. And still have.

PING PONG

25 JULY 2014

On Friday night, I attended a Ping Pong night organised by my work colleagues at London's Bounce. It's a really fun night and something that happens a couple of times a year. Everyone is organised into doubles teams and the evening consists of beer, good cheer and banter, as we all live through the highs and lows of winning and losing. Except I choose not to play.

I like to go along and be part of the social event but I can't bear team sports or competitive situations. I'm much happier witnessing the progress of others with a glass of wine in my hand, capturing the action on social media.

An interesting thing happens each time I go along to one of these things. I'm routinely asked why I'm not playing, if I wished I was, if I regret my decision, if I feel I'm missing out. Usually the questions come from just one or two people who can't believe I've opted out and are desperate to make me part of the game. Nope, I say, I'm happy with my choice.

I'm childfree-by-choice, as it happens, and my life is often like that Ping Pong night, complete with a continuous rolling sidebar of questions from friends and strangers, although they get less frequent as I get older and out of the baby-making zone.

I've always known I didn't want kids, even as a teenager, and although I have always been very clear on the decision, I have regularly 'checked in' with myself to make sure my head was still in agreement with my heart. There have been pressure points along the way – I had to have The Conversation with my husband-to-be about it in case he thought I'd change my mind. "I never say never," I said, "but as far as things stand now, I don't want them, and you need to be sure you want to be with me."

Then came the weddings-and-babies years of my thirties – the peer pressure was huge. "It's just what you do," friends said. The more they said that the more I questioned it. I'd never want to 'just do' anything that everyone else is doing just for the sake of it.

I loved my friends' babies but sometimes my enthusiasm for them was taken as a 'sign' that I was broody. There was one particular weekend where I was doing that couply thing of staying in a country cottage with a group of friends. One couple brought their adorable baby boy and I bounced him on my knee for pretty much the whole weekend. Looks passed among the group as if to say, "See? Finally she's joined us." I hadn't. I had just met a tiny person that I really liked being with. Looking back at the pictures still makes me smile. He was smily, fat-cheeked and gorgeous.

One by one, my friends had their children. Many of them struggled to conceive and being childfree, they felt able to tell me about their problems. I was so grateful not to have the all-encompassing urge to get pregnant, that I could hear their stories and comfort them as much as I could. It seemed as though they thought it was some sort of failure on their part, that they struggled to admit to each other, but could do so to me. Some friends admitted to me that they didn't realise they'd had a choice about having children, and that they hadn't expected the 'drudgery' of their post-natal lives. But then they threw themselves into it, happily, and had one or two more children. In for a penny, I suppose...

I did have a couple of wobbles during those years – mainly because having babies was what everyone was doing. My opting out of it was like choosing not to go to university, have a husband, buy a house – like not ticking a box in the tick-box life. But my gut instinct was right and I stuck to it.

There are possible underlying reasons why I don't want children, such as my parents dying early, that may be partly responsible for my decision. I do feel very strongly about not willingly inflicting that experience on another person, especially as an older parent. But perhaps there is also some truth in the other statement sometimes lobbed at me: "You just haven't met the right man yet."

The only time I've ever felt anything close to an urge to have a baby, it was because I had fallen deeply in love with a man. I think I must have a low-level 'water-table' of maternal hormones that were brought tantalisingly close to the surface during that time, but I'm grateful to my gut instinct, because that man turned out to be a colossal git.

Whenever I get the Sidebar of Questions, including the usual, "But you'd be a great mum!" I always say, "I'd make a great bus conductor, but I'm not here to do that either." I just know I'm not here to be a mother. Other people are, and they're great at it. I love seeing my friends raising their beautiful children and I salute them. I have loved accompanying my godson and his mother when he is at football, trampolining lessons or drumming on a kit in a music shop (he's brilliant at it: I call him "rock-godson"). It does give me joy and thank goodness I do have my friends' children in my life.

Someone once said to me that freedom was obviously the most important thing to me. At the time it didn't quite register. "Is it?!" I thought. I was still married at that point, but looking back, I was constantly making bids for freedom. My running times at weekends had got longer and longer as I plunged deeper into the Buckinghamshire countryside, on ever more circuitous routes that would wear me out. I was staying out after work more and more and taking all-day shopping trips on Saturdays. On holidays, I longed to disappear off over the horizon on my own. In retrospect, it was all pretty clear.

Yes, freedom is incredibly important to me. I long to have a Jack Russell in my life, but it would curb my freedom and would be unfair on the animal. I know it sounds ridiculous, but the same would apply to a baby. It would completely unfair on both of us if I had one.

Am I being selfish? I'm sure someone will tell me I am. I will admit openly that I do not want to live my life through someone else's – the things I've achieved have come relatively late in life and they've been hard won. If being selfish is making a decision that improves my life and avoids a disappointing one for another human being, then I'm happy to live with that.

And I do.

Because I can.

MEET THE PARENTS

21 JUNE 2015 – FATHER'S DAY

Another celebratory day dedicated to parenthood, and another chance for me to wallow, if I wanted to, in the double-whammy of not having any living parents and not being a parent. Mercifully for me, the latter was a choice.

I like to think about my dad on Father's Day, but I've decided to change the way I think about these days. I've decided to think about what is in my life, rather than what isn't. What is in my life is a group of friends, some, maybe most of whom are parents.

Some of them doing it on their own because their marriages broke down, some of them doing it on their own not knowing who donated the sperm to make their beautiful baby, some of them are in a family unit, some of them are far away, bringing up children in a different culture, some of them came into parenthood by mistake, some of them were trying for years to make it happen.

Even though I made the choice to be childfree, I am in a state of constant admiration for those who have gone there. I know that I could not go through the assault on my independence and selfhood but many of my friends do and they've emerged on the other side. Every time one of these days comes up I think about all of my friends and their transition into parenthood and how they have all done it differently.

Their children are now at the age where they are making their own transitions into secondary school, or preparing for GCSEs, or starting at university and I wonder how it must feel for the parents when their child first goes to school or leaves the family home for the first time.

I'll never know how that feels but if they are living their single lives vicariously through me, I'm living my family life vicariously through them. I like having an insight on what parenthood entails, I've just chosen not to go there. It does leave me with questions about the idea of being surrounded by a safety net of 'loved ones' and what that means for me, but I have made the choice to be a single unit so there it is. Every now and again I get invited into a family fold and I really enjoy it.

So, today I am focusing on who is in my life, not who isn't. No dad, but plenty of dads. And they're really cool. The ones sharing custody of children, the ones in the close-knit family, the ones who are single parents, the ones who are struggling a little bit with the adjustment to parental life. And of course, the ones who are in partnerships and still trying to be a dad.

One of the hopes I had for my ex-husband was that he would go off and get the chance to be a dad because I always thought he'd make a great one. I hope he did it because if there's one thing the world needs, it's great dads.

SECRET 5

YOU CAN GO ON HOLIDAY ON YOUR OWN

One of the greatest joys of my adult life is solo travel. A few months after I left my husband, I travelled to Thailand alone (twice) and since then I've flown solo to Turkey, Egypt, Costa Rica and India, returning to those countries many times in pursuit of complete freedom.

In recent times, curtailed by the two-year lockdowns of the coronavirus pandemic, this has morphed into solo hiking trips in the UK, beginning with the Isle of Wight coastal path and most recently, Anglesey, in my home country of Wales.

I am a coastal person. I grew up on the North Welsh coast and I live by the coast in Sussex now. I love the freedom of a limitless horizon. My ex-husband was coastal too, from the east coast of Scotland and we shared a love of adventure, going on road trips in Kenya, New Zealand and Namibia. I realised years later that he had been my 'adventure enabler', taking me as far as he could to those horizons but unable to accompany me to their limits. That was a bit I had to do by myself, and I'm still doing it.

Many people, mostly women, tell me I'm 'brave' for

striking out alone and I always laugh because it isn't the biggest act of bravery at all. The bravery is in the flying solo in the world at all, when seemingly everyone else is striving for coupledom. That is what will test your courage.

There is no doubt that I was scared on those first solo visits, especially to each new country because I didn't know what to expect. I came to regard those first holidays as 'exploratory missions' requiring at least a second trip – as it was I went to all those places I've listed at least twice and to Turkey, Egypt and India many times, until the places I was staying in felt like home. I had got to know the people there and got under the skin of tourism to find communities of people like me, searching for their own limitless horizons.

Be prepared for questions, people staring and sometimes being ignored. People are genuinely fascinated in a solo woman travelling, especially if she's over forty. I've been stared at by American women in Costa Rica, holding tightly onto their husbands, and ignored by hotel photographers who don't know what to do when a solo woman turns up on the steps into the hotel restaurant. But do what I did – make him take the photographs and ask him why he ignored you. He'll become a friendly face at dinner and give you the photos for free.

CONSCIOUSLY UNCOUPLING

20 JULY 2014

On July 13 2010, I booked my first holiday alone, in Thailand. It would turn out to be a momentous move. I and my then husband had agreed to split in May that year – I had initiated the split. We were sharing the same house, in separate rooms and I longed for freedom and to start leading my own life. I called Trailfinders and said, "Where can you take me?" and they suggested ten days in Phuket at a lovely resort. I booked it before I could think about it too much.

That was the first of six holidays I've been on, on my own. I am now a seasoned solo traveller, used to pacing my days to my own rhythm, not having to think about anyone else's likes, dislikes, lack of energy or enthusiasm. I can see everything I want to see, when I want to, for as long as I want to. It's gloriously liberating. Even a day out now, with friends, reminds me how much I end up compromising my own desires to fit in with theirs, and how much I long for that holiday space alone. But it didn't start like that.

Those first few days in Phuket, I was wretched. I seemed to be surrounded by happy couples, mooning over each other. Everywhere. That first night, I sobbed into my beautiful dinner and it heralded three days of the same pattern: bawling my eyes out throughout the night, dragging my piglet-eyed self to breakfast the next morning (thank god for shades) and recovering throughout the day on a sun-lounger at the end of a jetty with no one else on it.

I had travelled far away from home deliberately, because I knew I wouldn't be able to hop back on a plane if I couldn't stand it anymore. It worked. A combination of supportive texts from friends urging me to get out of the hotel and explore (and one particularly good one who reviewed the hotel's website and suggested a few trips and beauty treatments for me) made me do it. I sat at the hotel bar at Happy Hour, dressed nicely with a little makeup to hide the piglet eyes. I needed a couple of margaritas to give me the courage to leave the hotel and go into Patong – the 'Brighton' of Thailand.

I laughed when I tentatively stepped into a tuktuk only to find it took me about two minutes to get into town – I resolved to walk next time. Then I hit on a course of action that never fails to work abroad – find an Irish or Aussie pub and go sit at the bar with a drink. There was live music playing and I sat there, no one staring (except a British couple, which I've found is always the case) smiling into my Thai beer as I swung my legs on the bar stool. No one spoke to me that night but they did when I came back the next night, this time dressed in a more relaxed style in shorts and a vest. A crowd of Aussies took me under their wing. They couldn't believe I was on my own and to be honest, neither could I. I was forty-three and all my friends were holidaying with their partners.

Well, my partner for that holiday was Dougie. Aussie, Thai boxer, black-haired, hot-as-hell Dougie. Riding around on the back of his hired motorbike, I felt a sense of that freedom that I envy guys for – when you see gangs of them, shirts off, riding around Thai islands without a care in the world. (Do you ever see gangs of girls doing that?) I still envy those guys. The world is made for them and they rejoice in it.

The world is seemingly not made for a fortysomething woman who decides to leave her marriage (to a really nice guy) not to have children and go it alone. This blog is going to look at some of the unexpected things I've encountered since I've gone solo (they're pretty much all unexpected) from men my age assuming I want to trap them into coupledom, to women buying me congratulatory drinks at the bar; from dining alone to finding myself sandwiched between two Thai women on a tiny bike on New Year's Day. There's a story to tell, and I want to share mine.

Because I can.

FLYING SOLO

29 DECEMBER 2014

WELL HERE I AM, literally flying solo from Sharm El Sheikh in Egypt, at the end of another glorious holiday on my own.

I've got the routine down pat. From that first holiday in Thailand, where I spent days feeling sorry for myself in an exotic location, I'm now a veteran of the experience, knowing how to play it, how to pace my time and how to react when people question me about it.

Today I got questioned by one of the hotel's numerous managers: he had thought that by reading my book alone on the beach that I didn't like the hotel. Nothing could be further from the truth – feeling relaxed enough to do that on day one is pretty much my personal seal of approval. Why is reading alone seen as such an antisocial activity? This came on the heels of another hotel employee asking me why I was reading rather than relaxing – to him the two were very definitely exclusive – and later I was told that all the staff thought I was a doctor because I was wearing glasses and reading books. Wherever I go I am known as the 'lady with book' – people seem genuinely surprised that I read.

But like many solo travellers, the book is my travelling companion, my security blanket, my go-to item when I'm plunged into an unfamiliar setting. I can quickly immerse myself in a fictional (or non-fictional) world when I'm surrounded by couples and families on the beach, at dinner in a crowded restaurant, in a coffee shop filled with Egyptians or Turks. When a book is with me, I have a bubble to escape into, and I zone out all of the noise and activity around me. It's so much more than 'just a thing to do with your hands' when you're on your own.

I tend to punctuate my time on holiday by booking a few trips – this time to the White Canyon in Nuweiba (where you have to haul yourself out by a rope!) and a submarine trip to see fish on Napoleon Reef (I don't swim). This is a great way of meeting new people, especially if you're thrust into potentially life-threatening situations, as in the canyon.

What thrilled me on that trip was seeing an Egyptian couple bring along their one-year-old (beautiful Maryam) and entrust her safety completely to the guide. For most of the walk/climb through the canyon, he held her on his shoulders and she slept with her head on his. He even took her with him when he climbed out of the canyon using only the rope. The parents were mildly anxious, but not freaking out, as I would have been. It made me think about challenges and scary things, and how they're not so scary when you get up close to them. That guide held out his strong dark hand every time I exclaimed, "I'm scared!", and pulled me up over a boulder or tricky climb. I kept thinking, 'Well if he can do it with a baby on his head...'

The first time I came to Egypt I was scared: of the people, my perception of the culture and religion, the language. Everything. It didn't help that a Dahab shopkeeper spiked my tea when I went into his shop – I literally ran out and off to the hotel shuttle bus, vowing never to go back again. But I've gone back again and I've laughed at how normal it all seems because I'm not seeing it all through the veil of scariness. I walked past his shop, at night this time, and stopped to talk to other shopkeepers who've simply sold me something without hassling me (although the non-hassling ones are few and far between – I make a point of going into their shops. By the way, I don't think that shopkeeper intended to drug me – the tea had a mildly fuzzing effect that was probably intended to relax me into more shopping. He looked genuinely surprised when I ran out.)

[*later I realised this had been a self-induced panic attack*]

That first time in Dahab town, I swathed myself in a long dress and scarf around my head, so as not to 'stand out'. No wonder I was hassled. This time I noticed Egyptian girls (I didn't see many women over thirty) running around in jeans and jackets, hair streaming free. However, the best moment was spotting a convoy of Muslim girls on quad bikes heading into the desert, in full headgear. You go, girls.

From the Bedouin guy next to the hotel selling me Turkish coffee and giving me some bread to help him feed the birds in his tent, to the guy selling me boat trips, it didn't take long before I stopped thinking these people were just after me for something. Of course, they're selling their wares, but both guys took time to chat to me, to tell me about their lives and make me feel comfortable. Add to that the Egyptian couple in the canyon, who left an open invitation to their place in Cairo and emailed pictures they took of me wobbling and panicking up the canyon wall.

In many ways, the canyon trip represents the challenge of holidaying alone for me – I knew it would be beautiful-but-frightening. That I might fear for my life as I made my way through and wish I wasn't there at all, but then smile heartily over a Sakara beer that night and feel my soul enriched by the experience. I would want to do it again. And I do.

This brings me on to an experience I call The Rollercoaster. Each and every holiday alone does not go to plan. I never end up doing what I think I'm going to be doing on any given day and I've learned to ride the rollercoaster, wherever it may take me.

Four years ago, a terrible New Year's Eve in Thailand led to a wonderful New Year's Day, where I rode around Koh Samui on a bike, in between two Thai women who wanted to show me around. We eventually we went clubbing and had the time of our lives. I resolved then that New Year's Day is the new New Year's Eve.

The trick with The Rollercoaster is not to give up when things feel a bit grim. On your own at dinner one night? There'll be a party invite the next, or an unexpected meeting with an old friend in a bar in town ... or new one. Don't expect anything and everything will happen in its own good time. It always does, and it's just done it again. I love it. It's life.

The other trick is not to rely on anyone else for your plans. I once met two Australian sisters in Phuket and they promised hand on heart to come back after their trip to Phi Phi to spend the last day of my holiday with me. I looked forward to it so much and they never showed. But I did end up meeting an Indian air stewardess in a bar and we went clubbing together, so all was not lost.

The Rollercoaster. Part of me just wants to get on the waltzers, or even just the children's spinning teacups, and have a nice ride round with no thrills or spills. But then the lure of the unseen horizons over the top of the rollercoaster's peaks and loops are too much for me and I have to send myself there. It's always, always worth it.

An update on the subject of safety:

The only times I've particularly felt unsafe while travelling were when I had let my preconceptions about a country fuel my fears. I have been holidaying alone for nearly five years and taking those first steps into a Thai town, a Turkish city or an Egyptian village are incredibly scary. I once allowed myself to believe I'd been drugged in a shop in Dahab by a shopkeeper, when in fact it was probably a panic attack brought on by fear. Similarly in Kenya, a scary group of men on motorbikes I kept seeing when out running on my own turned out to be a taxi rank. Of course, women are viewed differently in these countries, and it would be stupid to not be on your guard, but as someone who is fully aware of the potential hazards, I walk in confidently and try to see things as they really are.

I always watch men on holiday with a sense of envy. They are completely free to roam wherever they like, without much fear for their safety. There is a reason why some of the best travel books are written by men and not by women, and I long to be as free as those guys riding round Thailand on motorbikes without a care in the world. But I know my situation isn't the same as theirs and have to adapt my experiences to fit.

My advice to any solo woman traveller would be, be aware of the potential hazards by reading up before you go. Beware of scaremongering features in the media and opt for sensibly written guides from *Lonely Planet* or *Rough Guides*. Yes, it's wrong to have to restrict your behaviour or clothing options in certain settings, but it does make sense. I do agree with this article in terms of trusting your gut instinct when it comes to certain situations. If something or someone is making you feel uncomfortable, get out of there, even if you discover later that your fears were unfounded.

I think it's a shame that many women will read scaremongering articles in the media, and be put off from travelling alone and discovering the world. Many people would prefer women to stay in a domestic setting and not discover the joy of solo travel. Yes, you should know the hazards and look at other intelligent travellers' tips on staying safe, but never let it stop you from taking those steps into the wider world.

HOW TO GO ON HOLIDAY ON YOUR OWN

29 JUNE 2015

I SEEM to be part of a zeitgeist for solo travel, with more and more people than ever opting to take their vacations on their own, even if they're in a couple. I've been doing it for five years now, and I'm addicted. On my own, I can holiday at my own pace and I can choose to be with other people, or not. I've found the freedom exhilarating.

The first holiday, to Thailand, was a huge test for me. I spent the first three days in the hotel, too scared to go outside. But once I did, encouraged by friends texting me, I found the world was waiting for me.

Here are my top tips on solo travel:

Start just outside your comfort zone

Book your first solo holiday in an all-inclusive hotel, or wherever you feel safe. Just flying far away on your own is stressful enough so be nice to yourself by booking a safe haven at the other end. You can then be more adventurous when you're there but have a base to return to. I asked Trailfinders to find me a lovely hotel in Thailand, and when I got there, I got upgraded to a seafront room. I then used the hotel as a base for trips, so I could see the lie of the land.

Book lots of trips

If you're not on a group holiday (I choose not to join those) then book day trips. My favourite thing is a boat trip and I've met so many great people while on them, often women who are on their own. I tend to alternate between days by the pool/beach and day trips. It gives the holiday a bit of pace and gives you a chance to talk to people over the course of a day, and potentially meet them again as a dinner companion.

Let preconceptions go

Most of us arrive in countries with preconceptions about the culture and we need to form our own. You will find that the things you find most alien, or are scared of, become ridiculously normal and tame after a few days. Beware of scaremongering. Most people are too afraid to go away on their own and look for reasons why they shouldn't. Research your destination and know what you're in for but draw your own conclusions about it.

Prepare for the Rollercoaster

A solo holiday is a rollercoaster. You will experience days when an unexpected meeting or event propels you into a state of high excitement, followed by days where nothing happens and you start to feel sorry for yourself. Know that it will happen and embrace the Rollercoaster. Don't rely on other people for your holiday highs - they will happen when you least expect, and usually just at the point you wish you hadn't gone away on your own.

Take lots of books

Books are the solo travel companion you can rely on in any setting. At the airport, on the beach, at lunch or dinner on your own, even Happy Hour in the hotel. Have your book with you and you can lose yourself in it and stop focusing on your alone-ness. Make sure you have enough to see you through the holiday and a potential flight delay.

Share your experience

If you're like me, you want to share your experience on social media, and use it as a travelogue and a form of companionship. Wifi-allowing, think of your holiday as a window onto the world that you can share with others – there is a whole community doing it on Instagram, for instance, and you can be one of them.

Enjoy the journey

I've found that the journey to my destination on my own is an adventure in itself. From the moment you step out of your door on the way to the airport or train station, you are doing something amazing. Most people can't even go for a walk on their own.

Realise that people are envious of you

You will find, at lunch, dinner, or any other 'social' occasion on holiday, that people will look at you. They won't be able to believe that you are brave enough to go on holiday on your own. But you are. And you can smile back at them, safe in the knowledge that they wish they were you.

PURA VIDA!

14 AUGUST 2016

It's almost six years to the day that I first embarked on one of my solo holidays. I deliberately chose somewhere far away (Thailand) so I wouldn't be able to chicken out and fly home ahead of time. I found the first few days really challenging but once I found my groove I couldn't wait to go back again. And I did, a few months later.

Since then I've found a couple of places I love – Bodrum in Turkey and Dahab in Egypt– and visited them over and over again because I feel so comfortable there. This year, though, I felt like trying somewhere new, not least because I can't currently fly to Dahab (flights aren't currently going to Sharm-el-Sheikh from the UK) and Bodrum has been at the centre of the refugee crisis in the last year or so. I didn't feel right to go there for pleasure.

Costa Rica has recently loomed onto the UK holiday horizon, partly because of the reintroduction of direct flights there from tour operators like Thomson (they started last November). I'd seen a friend's holiday pictures over Christmas and thought it looked like the perfect destination for me – beautiful beaches, lush forests, interesting flora and fauna. I booked it before I could think about it too much.

My destination was Tamarindo, a surf town in the north west on the Pacific coast. At this time of year, the rainy season, the Pacific side is the driest, and July gives a short respite in the rains, that the locals call 'Little Summer'. It rains a bit, but not nearly as much as it does between May and November in other months. What the rainy season does give you is a daily spectacular sunset, and Tamarindo is famous for it. Nary a day goes by without one lighting the curious cloud formations in a unique, glorious way.

Towards the end of my holiday I decided to take a 'sunset cruise' that hilariously turned into a 'storm cruise' with a dash back to the shore and being told to run for it across the beach because someone had been killed by lightning the week before. During my two-week trip, the lightning strike happened, plus a guy got his leg chewed off by a croc in Tamarindo estuary (he was walking where he shouldn't) and a volcano erupted. Costa Rica is certainly 'lively' when it comes to natural-world news.

Tamarindo is happily also famous for its party atmosphere. One of the things I need when I'm away on my own is access to lively nightlife. I've found I can lose myself in local bars and clubs, whereas it's more difficult in a quiet restaurant. I need lots of people around at night, and Tamarindo (or Tamagringo, as the locals refer to it) doesn't disappoint. As the guides suggest, it has something of a 'spring break' feel about it, with a range of bars catering to the American surf crowd.

I preferred the local 'Tico' places – like Pacifico, where you can't stand still for five seconds without someone whizzing you round the dance floor to the latest salsa hit. And then there's the Crazy Monkey Bar, where everyone heads on a Friday night, split between a Gringo and a Tico dancefloor. Guess which one I headed to? Yep – Tico every time. Much more fun, and more relaxed. Beware the free shots given to ladies though – Guaro chilli shots are pretty lethal.

I've realised that what I really like is a hotel base, near to a lively town, but just out of the way enough to get away. The Esplendor Tamarindo is perched on the hill above the town and has spectacular views of the sunset from a swim-up bar. Howler monkeys fight for territory in the trees around the infinity pool and the tree-lined hills behind the hotel are filled with birdsong all day. Every room faces the ocean so it's a place where no one feels disgruntled with their room choice.

The hotel/town situation reminded me very much of my first solo experience in Thailand. There, I was staying in an extremely romantic hotel, upgraded to a seaview, but I had access to a nearby party town that was only two minutes away. I could leave behind the romantic couples looking at the sunset and head into town for fun.

I laughed when I realised the similarity, but not so much when I realised how daunting it is going to a completely new continent so far away, on your own. I'd forgotten, in the years of repeat visits to Bodrum and Dahab, that it's fairly stressful not knowing how things work. I quickly realised what was going to happen – it would take me several days, or even a week, to get into the swing of things, and then I'd want to book a repeat visit so I could go back and do it properly. And that is exactly what did happen.

Luckily for me, I had a bit of a false start to the holiday, meeting a guy on his own in the hotel. He had found out lots of local information via an American guy who had retired there, and it gave me an instant solo-holiday boost. He was also great to hang out with, and we ended up touring the local bars one night, in what appeared to be a live Bacardi advert. We packed it all in – karaoke, salsa, house music – it was one of those nights. When he left a few days later I came crashing down with the realisation that I was on my own and I'd have to make my own fun. I really did wallow for a bit and it brought back those first wretched days in Thailand. But I did what I did back then, and booked some trips to shake off the gloom.

And then I met Nolberto the tour guide. My first trip was a guided group hike to Rincon De La Vieja – one of the four active volcanoes. Nolberto, like many of the Tico guides I came across, was well drilled in the history, culture and politics of his country. There is no army, he told us proudly. The money is spent instead on health and education, and education is compulsory for 7–12-year-olds. He told us that the first mile or so of the hiking track into the forest is paved so that people in wheelchairs could enjoy the experience.

I realised why people want to live in Costa so much. Everything is focused on a better quality of life – '*pura vida*' – the 'pure life' statement that punctuates pretty much everything a Tico says.

During a post-hike visit to some hot springs, an American woman asked me what I thought about Brexit. They all did, every time I met one. And all but one was hugely sympathetic to the 48% Remain voters and worried about the threat posed to the US by Donald Trump. Hillary just HAS to get in, said one. I said it might be a good idea to prepare for the worst, just in case. So many of us in the UK had been caught out by complacency and it would be wise to go there in your head before it happened.

Mostly I get scowled at by women in couples on these sorts of holidays. They appear to think I pose some sort of threat, and their partners pick up on it and are invariably too scared to talk to me. A few times I got approached by women who were genuinely interested in what I was doing on my solo holiday and were comfortable enough in their marriages to include me in their family group. I really appreciated it. Thanks, ladies.

I've found, especially now I'm older, that I also get ignored by staff in restaurants and beach clubs. I'm told it's because they can get more money out of couples and groups, but it felt as though it was the 'cloak of invisibility' that descends upon women after the age of 46. Seeing a waiter who had previously ignored me, running after a group of young surf girls at Lola's, kind of confirmed that for me. Mind you, that was during my low point, so I was probably more sensitive than normal. Lola's is a fantastic restaurant on the glorious Playa Avellanas – highly recommended. Especially the free Imperial Beer you get when you tell the waiter off...

Anyway, back to Nolberto. He'd given me his card on the trip and as he's freelance, I thought I'd book him to go on my next trip to Monteverde. I'd tried booking a group trip in town, but they seemed to run only when they could amass enough people and I didn't want to wait and miss out. On the spectacular drive there (it's a cloud forest in the mountains), Nolberto had a habit of shouting, "Vámonos!" every time he overtook a slow vehicle (which was a lot). I started shouting it as well, and it made us laugh so much. He was great fun.

I realised how great it was to have a private guide on that day. It happened to be Guanacaste Day – the day that people in the north-western region I was in celebrate their annexation from Nicaragua. And boy, do they celebrate it. On the way back from Monteverde we stopped at Bar Y La Griega near Santa Cruz and they had a cimarrona band playing. It was a group of high-school boys standing outside the bar in the dark playing a frenzied mariachi-style music (which is usually accompanied by dancing puppets). One of things I'd never have witnessed if I'd been on a group tour.

Nolberto also tracked down sloths for me – I couldn't visit the country and not see at least one. We travelled back to the volcano region to Finca Verde Lodge in Bijagua, which turned out to be a little gem of a place with hardly any visitors. We saw three small sloths nestled high up in the cecropia trees they love so much and were told that they only come down about twice a week for toilet purposes.

Amazingly, one popped down while I was having my lunch and Nolberto passed it over to me to hold. It is simply one of the most beautiful moments of my life. It felt like a hairy baby, this eight-month-old three-toed sloth, that naturally curls its arms around you for a cuddle. He was stoned, of course, from the cecropia leaves, but his smile came from being a three-toed sloth. They all have them. And quite frankly, I don't blame them.

[*I later realised that the animal was probably extremely frightened and I would advise watching the animals in the wild at a distance.*]

Nolberto also encouraged me to zipline whilst at Selvatura Park in Monteverde. I was really scared but I knew I'd regret it if I didn't do it. It comprises twelve 'flights' across eighteen platforms and once I'd (literally) got into the swing of it, I was dying to do it again. I had to be 'accompanied' across a few flights by random guys – you had to do some of them in pairs. Thanks to the three guys who gallantly placed their legs around my waist without even knowing my name.

As with Thailand, I'm now feeling an overwhelming urge to return to Costa Rica. I wish I'd spent way more time in the mountains and done a lot more hiking. I wish I'd spent more time partying in the evenings and not so much going to bed early. I wish I'd spent more time with the locals. I wish I'd gone one step further on my first attempt at snorkelling in the sea but panicking in a life vest was as far as I got, and that was a lifetime achievement (I can't swim).

I suppose it's like that old adage about leaving the dinner table still wanting more.

I'll be back, Costa Rica, I'll be back...

[*I did go back, I learned to swim, I spent time in the mountains and did a lot more hiking – and partying with the locals!*]

SECRET 6

SINGLE LIFE ISN'T PERFECT (BUT NEITHER IS COUPLEDOM)

THIS IS the chapter where I admit that single life isn't all a bed of towel sculptures in fancy hotel rooms. I've already told you about the solo holiday rollercoaster and the newsflash is: single life in general has its own fairground ride. Just like life with a partner, it has its ups and downs, but the good news is that you're in charge of them. If, as with the holidays, you can stand back and witness the wave, knowing that any downward curve is going to be followed by an upward one, you can withstand the emotional stress that comes with it.

When you are leading a solo life you have the benefit of being more in tune with your self – and by 'self' I mean that inner part of you, the one that drives your gut instinct. You will develop awareness of your own emotional triggers as time goes on and find ways of managing them, whether that's through yoga, therapy, hiking, HRT and giving up drinking (like me) or long, hot baths, cold-water swims or a solo trip to the cinema (which I highly recommend – no one to tell you they hate the movie you've just loved).

I have found solace in social media during my own low

solo moments – often around birthdays, Bank Holidays or even just Sundays: days that are earmarked by society for spending with 'loved ones'. As someone who lost both parents fairly young (at ten and thirty-two) and doesn't have close family connections, this phrase – loved ones – can be triggering. Thankfully, I have found out who my real loved one is, and I will talk about them in the next chapter.

HOME ALONE

18 DECEMBER 2014

Last year I decided to do Christmas alone in London. It felt right – like I could handle it. After three years of either being away on holiday or throwing myself into charity work for Crisis, I thought 'I can do this'. I can be in my flat, on Christmas Day, on my own, and just be.

I planned it – I knew what the day would entail and I was really looking forward to it. I'd go for an early morning run; I'd make coffee and a hearty breakfast; I'd open my presents while watching something crap on TV, sitting next to my beautifully decorated tree. How hard could it be? I'd be seeing one of my friends whom I'd met at Crisis later that day and enjoying a Christmas dinner with her and her flat-mate. All good.

But oh my god. Those hours. Those long, long hours.

It really started going wrong on Christmas Eve. I'd left work full of seasonal joy (and prosecco) at around 4pm, slightly thinking that there might be a post-work pub moment. There wasn't. Everyone went home. I went along to HMV and bought myself a boxset of something – can't remember what. I went home, shrouded in increasing gloom.

Again, I'd thought there'd be some spontaneous socialising to be done back at the ranch – nothing doing. Everyone had, in the words of one neighbour, "fucked off for Christmas." This is what people do (even though most of my local friends and neighbours are Jewish.) But it was ok – I still had my plan and my dinner to go to.

It started so well – it was one of those crisp, sunny mornings and I ran a few laps of my local park saying, "Merry Christmas!" to passers-by who were walking dogs or hurrying to a family gathering. The endorphin rush got me through the next hour or so, as I made breakfast and slowly opened my presents.

I'd made a pact with myself not to look at social media, because I knew what I'd see – pictures of cosy Christmas family mayhem and drunken antics – but let's face it, I broke the pact within a couple of hours.

I know what the reality of a family Christmas is because I've been there. The seasonal cheer lasts about four hours before the rows, the tears, the sniping, the wishing-I-was-anywhere-but-there feelings kick in, especially when they involve in-laws. But still, I believed the Facebook hype – that everyone was having the BEST time. Of course they're bloody not.

To give myself credit, I lasted about four hours before giving in to the wallowing. My first mistake was 'seeing no harm' in opening one of my stack of prosecco bottles, just for a 'glass or two' over lunch. My second was to start watching an extremely romantic film that a friend had bought me on DVD for Christmas. There's a reason why they don't show these movies on Christmas Day – stick with the comedies, people.

Let's just say that for the ensuing four hours after those mistakes were made, I descended into a pit of gloom so deep it resembled the Mines of Moria. It was like slowly dying and being reborn as I emerged from the pit at around 5pm, blinking, into the Christmas lights of my friend's flat, and having a glass of champagne thrust into my hand. Little did the people I was with know, as I joined in laughing at the *Morecambe & Wise Christmas Special* and munching on pigs in blankets.

The memory of those few dark hours is enough to see me heading off on holiday this Christmas and New Year, alone, but not 'doing Christmas'. I know I'll be surrounded by 'entertainment' staff in the hotel, wearing Santa hats and trying to get me to be Christmassy but I'll be relishing the non-Christianness of the location and reading a book on the beach. Why don't the people in these hotels realise you're there to get away from Christmas, not recreate it in their country?

I remember my first Christmas alone in Thailand, and a well-meaning couple who forced me to join them in a bar, because I 'couldn't be alone on Christmas Day' – except I could and I wanted to be. Out there I was absolutely fine on my own – it was only other people's perceptions that made me feel crap about it. And that was the year I had the worst New Year's Eve EVER on my own, but the BEST New Year's Day, on a motorbike in between two Thai women, touring round Koh Samui, followed by all-night clubbing.

That's when I realised.

The real fun happens on the day when you least expect it.

. . .

SPOILT ROTTEN

14 MARCH 2015

It's my birthday today, and like every year, I brace myself for the inevitable "hope someone is spoiling you rotten" comment. Every time I see it on other people's Facebook messages I think of them sitting on a throne wearing a towelling robe, attended by manservants who are bringing champagne, cakes and all manner of gifts while they gorge on everything in sight.

This has never happened to me in my whole history of birthdays (except maybe the time I turned eight and my parents had bought me a garden swing). Even while I was married it was never a Spoilt Rotten situation. More often than not, i was frogmarched round a shopping mall in Reading in search of something he could buy me. Exhausting.

Anyway, now I'm free and single, this is even less likely to happen and I'm largely ok with that. But last year, the comment came and I got really upset about it and railed on social media. "Just exactly do you think is going to spoil me rotten, eh? Who?" There is no secret Spoiling Rotten Fella who pops out of the woodwork on the day to make me breakfast in bed and whisk me off to Paris, people. There are no 'loved ones' to bring me a handmade card and make me blow out candles on a badly iced cake. I promptly took myself out shopping and splurged.

Last year, I did allow myself to wallow a little bit in the unfairness of it all. Until the day of my party, that is, which of course had been arranged by me. As friends turned up, laden with smiles, flowers, gifts and hugs, one friend whispered in my ear, "Spoilt rotten, I think."

And that's when I decided I had been.

This year, I remembered the phrase again. It came up on a radio show I was listening to, where a guest described being "*spoilt rotten by my loved ones.*" The old familiar feeling washed over me as I realised I was entering the Birthday Zone again, and someone might inadvertently say it again. "*I'm ready for you,*" I thought.

Then something happened. Last week I had a difficult situation to deal with and I've been overwhelmed by the show of support and love from all the good people in my life. Neighbours have rallied round me, friends have texted and called regularly to check I'm ok and people have taken time out of their busy lives to talk things through with me and offer advice.

Yes, I've been spoilt rotten yet again. And by real loved ones who never cease to amaze me with their heartfelt support for me.

So happy birthday to me. But really, guys, today is definitely all about you.

VENICE, VIDI, VICI

19 JUNE 2017

LAST WEEKEND I did something I've been wanting to do for years – go back to Venice. It was twenty-five years ago that I was first bewitched by the place, swearing I'd only go back for a romantic break with someone 'special'. That person didn't rock up, so goddammit, I went there by myself. I booked a cool, boutique hotel, planned my four days out using *Lonely Planet*, and re-entered the fantasy world of the city.

What I'd forgotten is that it's like entering a restaurant on a perma-Valentine's Night. The place is festooned with love and lovers, now taking 'kelfies' – my made-up word for kissing selfies. In front of every building, work of art or *bario* serving spritz ... there they were. I didn't really notice it last time I was there – I was too entranced with the place. Also, I was young enough to think I'd have my time there to do that. Lol.

So really, what I was doing was the Iron Woman Challenge of all solo holidays. Going to the most romantic place in the world as a middle-aged woman on her own. "*I can totally do this!*" I thought. And I did. Kind of.

I managed to dodge the rose-thrusting touts around St Mark's square, and chuckled when I heard an American woman behind me cry, "Do I LOOK like I'm with anyone??" That's the thing when you're a female solo traveller. You suddenly realise that you're surrounded by them. We're quite well-camouflaged, actually. No one suspects the woman blending into the surroundings looking like she's just waiting for someone, but we see each other very clearly, emerging from the scene. And there are more and more of us every year, it seems.

Even at the airport I'd gone to the champagne bar and made eye-contact with at least three other women doing the same thing as me: treating ourselves to a lovely glass before jetting off, because we could. I spoke to one of them and she was going to Berlin, but not before sneezing all over me and giving me a cold three days later. Thanks, love.

Anyway, on my first night I was full of the joy of being alone and free in the most beautiful city in the world. I'd planned a walk around San Marco, which would culminate in a spritz at a bar I'd been recommended. Of course, Venice being Venice, I couldn't find it so I found an accommodating restaurant – the Rosa Rossa – who found me a table tucked away outside. I smiled at my good fortune and ordered a spritz.

Fifteen minutes passed and couples were starting to surround me. They appeared to be being served promptly so I reminded the waiter (he seemed to be the manager) that I'd been waiting for fifteen minutes. He broke out in what can only be described as operatic ritual humiliation of me in front of the other customers. Waving his arms around, he remonstrated with me, shouting that I'd only been waiting for five minutes and couldn't I see that they were busy and now, you see? Here is the drink you've been waiting for. *Prego, PREGO!*

I died a little in my seat. I also sat there for about five minutes choking back tears. He came back out to take my food order and instead of doing what I should have done – stormed off – I told him I'd order if he promised not to shout at me. It was the worst meal I've ever had in Italy, for so many reasons. The couple next to me looked shocked.

Thinking about it, what annoyed him about me was probably that I was the least important of his customers, but the one that ventured to complain. Had I been in a couple, I'm sure I'd have been served immediately. Had I been a girl of twenty-four, as I had been the last time I visited, I think he'd have been all over me. But me, just sitting there, at forty-nine, with no man or baby to make 'sense' of me, just got his goat.

It happened again on my return boat trip to the airport. The boat driver shouted at me for trying to pay at the wrong moment. I teared up again. So this is what happened in twenty-five years – I've gone from being catcalled to shouted at. I'm in the way.

Don't get me wrong, in between those moments, the weekend was a dream of renaissance art and architecture, of *La Traviata* in a palazzo on the Grand Canal and Vivaldi in a frescoed church. It was cicchetti and wine in a tucked-away street *bario* and a pistachio gelato next to a fantasy scene of sparkling waterways and winking gondoliers. It was everything I remembered the first time, but much more. And I'm going to go back.

And when I go back I'm going to remember the conversation I had with a woman who was visiting the city with her husband. He'd gone off to do something else and she'd taken a seat next to me in a bar and was taking a breather with a beer and a cigarette. I told her about my solo-travelling thing and why I'd got into that and she suddenly blurted out that she too was wishing she was on her own, and that she was thinking about leaving her husband. She probably only told me because I was a complete stranger, but I did start to wonder about all the kelfie-taking love-puppies I'd seen in gondolas. How many of them were wishing they were with someone, or no one, else?

I remembered feeling like that on numerous holidays, even my honeymoon, and felt glad that at least I was free of that. Free of scanning every place I went for the guy I was 'supposed' to be with. It's exhausting, and at the very least, unfair on the person you are actually with.

So Venice. I came, I saw, I conquered. I am so in love with you that I don't think I can leave it at that. You can make me feel elated and transcendent, but you can also make me feel like dirt on your shoe.

But at least I feel alive in your presence.

SECRET 7

THE GREATEST RELATIONSHIP YOU'LL EVER HAVE IS WITH YOURSELF

YES, I know this is a phrase that's bandied around on wellness Instagram accounts along with '*you are enough*' and '*live laugh love*'. I'm a yoga teacher now so forgive me if I sound a little yogi from time to time. But, the greatest lesson I learned from my training in India is the one in which I learned that love resides in us already. It isn't gifted to us by someone else – it is an essential part of our being.

My teacher, Sudhir Rishi, told me this when I asked him why yogis always say '*You are loved.*' I'd often think, by whom? What if there was no one around to offer you the love you needed? Who were the loved ones doing the loving?

His reply blew me away:

"Love is the nature of the self. It's in us. It's not coming from somewhere else. When the mind is disturbed, we don't experience that love. But, in the presence of some people, our mental blocks get cleared – we experience that love and we think it's

coming from them. A mother experiences that love from a child, parents experience it from their children, partners experience it from each other. But what is happening is that in their presence, the mind and heart are being cleared. The clouds go away and you experience the sun. The sun is always shining and so are love and joy, our true nature. Even if someone has no close family members, they can experience that love in their work, their passions, their friends."

I don't think any idea or concept has had such a profound effect on me as this simple truth from Indian philosophy, or Hinduism, as it's called in the West. Growing up in the West, we are taught that the original self is sinful, not joyful. I was brought up Catholic, so I felt particularly sinful and carried that guilt around with me for most of my life. And then, I asked the question to end all questions, and the answer was simply: You are love.

It's you, dear reader. This is the love you've been looking for and it's been inside you all this time crying out for recognition. In Indian philosophy we are taught that our essential joyful, loving nature becomes shrouded by the emotional clouds of adult life – there is a reason why children appear unshrouded (if their lives are not problematic, of course). It made me see children in a wholly different way, as literal bundles of joy.

I had shrouded my inner joy with a stressful career, an unhappy marriage, the grief of lost parents and the anaesthetic of alcohol. But as I started to peel away these elements from my life, I found it again, and you can see it emerging in the following blog posts.

ALL BY MYSELF

7 JUNE 2015

I'VE RECENTLY STARTED USING Periscope – a new app that allows you to broadcast live from your phone. Your followers are notified when you begin broadcasting and you can see them join you as you hold your phone camera at whatever it is you want to show them. They can comment and 'heart' your footage.

Today I went for a walk on Hampstead Heath and decided to broadcast from there, once I could get a good enough signal. I was taken aback by one follower, who asked me if I was really walking 'all by myself' and why did I not have friends with me for 'talks'. Quite apart from the strange phrasing, I was surprised that this was even an issue. To me, doing things on my own is just a way of life – a freedom, rather than a sadness. I know I can call friends to join me but I choose to be alone sometimes, thinking my own thoughts, just taking things in on my own, without anyone else's viewpoint to skew it.

Their comments reminded me of how far I've come. There was a time when, like lots of people, I would hardly do anything on my own. I wouldn't dream of going to the cinema, to a lecture, or even a gallery on my own, let alone a pub or club, or a foreign country. Now I do all of them, all the time, and I feel liberated. I can do exactly what I want, when I want, without having to rely on someone else being available, or wanting to do the same thing. I love spending time with my friends, but they don't have to always be there. Plus I always have social media if I fancy some 'talks'.

Thinking about it, though, I've always gone on solo walks. As one could in the seventies, I roamed around on my own in the Welsh countryside from about the age of eleven. No one thought anything of it, then. I used to walk through field after field to get to the local church (St David's in Pantasaph), roam around there for a bit, and walk back. I definitely met a few 'wanderers' on the way but we would just pass each other and not blink an eye. I'd play solo in a disused lime quarry which would probably be surrounded by a '*keep out*' fence now. If another kid was around, fine, but I made my own entertainment.

As a teenager, I roamed the moors near our house with our Jack Russell terrier and pretended I was Cathy about to meet my Heathcliff. I had, and still have, a very romantic imagination and it is possible that other people would've reminded me that I was still in the real world. I used to love looking at a field disappearing over the horizon and wondering what was over the top. In a way, I didn't want to know that there was just a hedge and another field. My mind filled in the blanks.

It's only recently that I've started walking again, solo, building in walks in and out of London, depending on where I'm working. I even walked to a party in Soho last Friday, taking my nice shoes in my bag. Until today, I'd forgotten that this was what I used to do all the time in my youth. Walk, walk and walk. Just me. No 'talks'.

Sometimes I have a whole day, which I refer to as a 'Wandering the Earth Day', where I just walk and commune with myself, and look around me at everything that's going on, often recording it on Instagram, Twitter, and now, Periscope. I see lots of couples, families, groups of friends, enjoying each other's company, or not. I pick up snippets of conversation, and I observe all-but-hidden behaviour. For instance, on Friday night, I noticed a lesbian couple dropping hands as they passed by a busy pub and I felt sad that they felt the need to do that. I'm not sure I'd notice that if I was with someone else.

There really is something special about just being on your own in the world. It can feel lonely sometimes, but that really is just a state of mind and I can always call someone if I don't fancy a good wallow in it. I look at people that can't do anything without someone else being by their side and think they're the ones that are missing out. Again and again, I think of the therapist who once told me that freedom was the most important thing for me.

And again and again, he was absolutely right.

BECAUSE I'M HAPPY

9 FEBRUARY 2016

I'M WRITING this ahead of Valentine's Day, because normally at this point the fear and dread has set in. I've never been keen on being in a pink, heart-festooned restaurant even when I was in a couple, but it's even worse when you're not. At least this year, VD (oops, did I just write that?) has the good sense to be on a Sunday, so we can all avoid the flower deliveries to the office and the smug carriers of said flowers on the train home. Normally, I'd be contemplating a day inside my flat, binge-watching something, and binge-eating something else.

But this year, I'm not. It doesn't actually matter anymore. I used to get all het up about this stuff, but that moment has passed. I know VD is a mostly sham experience, but hey – lots of my friends are in love, or have found love, so it's fine if they want to celebrate it. Hell, I'll even celebrate it with them (in a social-media sense).

I have found real love here and there in my life, but never for very long. I think the most I've managed is a few months. I remember the feeling it creates... That heady delight in everything, where you want to skip down the road and hand out flowers to small children and the elderly. You find yourself marvelling at the minute detail of the world and being kind to people on the Tube. I remember feeling like I wanted to pirouette down the street (dance training comes in handy) and sing, "I'm in love ... with a pretty wonderful boy!" from *West Side Story*.

The thing is, I'm feeling a bit like that right now. There's no romance in my life, although I do see a couple of guys occasionally. They make me feel happy when I'm with them because there's no pressure for it to be anything than what it is. I think I make them happy too. As a friend says to me quite often, "It is what it is, Babe." This has turned out to be my life mantra.

It's been coming on now for a few months. I have found a job that I love and people I love working with. I'm being collaboratively creative in a way that hasn't happened for years and it is making me so happy.

I have found myself letting old grudges gently slide (well, nearly all of them). I've realised people are just humans like me, imperfect and just trying their best. Might as well just all get along while we're here, eh? Why make it worse for ourselves?

I've found myself helping a variety of people on public transport and smiled at the surprise on their faces. I remember the last time I felt like this and it was a love affair that did it – it made me want to be kinder to people. How lovely that it can be done even without another person being involved. Who knew that all it required was just to feel genuinely happy in your own skin? I don't think I've ever felt like this.

So here I am, nearly forty-nine, single, feeling happy in my skin. And yes, I'm just as amazed as you probably are. It's not supposed to happen, is it? Women my age are meant to be surrounding themselves with cats and growing hairy warts on their faces. Instead, I'm striding out to work with a spring in my step, booking solo adventures abroad and saying howdy doody to surprised old people in north-west London. I've even given up dieting and don't feel the need to drown any sorrows in booze. I even spent Christmas in the UK, without feeling like I needed to get on a flight somewhere. Anywhere...

I've noticed for a while now that more people are smiling at me, in general. I think it's because my face is set in one (for a while I thought I had a 'little something' on my cheek). I've particularly enjoyed exchanging smiles with women when I'm out and about, mainly because smiling at men can often get you in trouble. And I think women SHOULD smile at each other more. There's way too much scowling for my liking.

So, if this post is making you gag with all its sickly sweetness, bear in mind that on Sunday, I might be celebrating the fact that you've found your own sickly sweet love. And I truly think that's great because I've felt its awesomeness.

But I'm afraid the old cliché is a cliché for a reason: because it's true.

In the words of Whitney Houston, learning to love yourself is the greatest love of all.

Happy Valentine's Day to me, and to all you lovers out there.

Mwah!

FAREWELL TO MY FORTIES

14 MARCH 2017

ANOTHER DECADE HAS ENDED and I am thinking back to those months just after I turned forty, when my mindset completely changed about who I was and what I wanted out of life.

I stood and took a selfie of myself in a hotel room in Cannes, in a Mediterranean Blue maxi dress, looking nervous but excited about the night ahead. That night changed everything. Coming back to London, I knew everything had to be different. And it was.

Thank you, forties, for letting me find out who I truly am; letting me explore my independence, my sexuality, my freedom, my voice, my self.

I look back at the 43-year-old who left a marriage and set out on that first holiday on her own to Thailand, who found herself flying round an island on the back of a motorbike with a black-haired boy and laughing.

I think about the person who stood in a bar alone, having a drink bought for her by a shocked woman (who went back to her husband eager to tell him what she'd done).

There is a scene where a woman buys a flat of her own in a golden building in a new place that turns out to be her real home.

There are beautiful young men who've appeared, grinning and eager, curious about the world, and even more curious about her.

I'm watching a woman reading on a beach in Dahab, watching the sun rise and fall behind shadowy mountains, smiling to herself about the evening ahead. She goes back to the hotel to write a blog post, because writing has become a way of processing her days and recording her experience. Maybe no one will read it, but it doesn't matter.

There is a woman who finally realises that shrinking her body is not the way of happiness. That being strong and in the world, taking up space, is the way she needs to be, and that there is nothing better than walking – walking along a coastal path or through a rainforest – to put her mind at rest.

Perhaps most surprisingly of all, there is a woman who realises she has something to say and has the confidence to say it. It's only taken forty or fifty years to get there. Yes, it might scare off some of the men she meets, but actually, that's fine. If they can't deal, they can't deal. She has friends who can.

So now I'm fifty and I need to stop talking about myself in the third person. It's here, and I'm excited and not afraid. I know how to do it – I worked it all out in my forties.

Let's do this.

WHITE HORSE

11 FEBRUARY 2018

> Maybe some women aren't meant to be tamed. Maybe they just need to run free until they find someone just as wild to run with them.
>
> *SEX AND THE CITY*

Every day in Agonda village, south Goa, a white horse walks slowly from her home through the streets. She heads down to the beach where she will walk slowly from back and forth along the shoreline until sundown. Throughout the day, she stops off at a beach hut or two for a slurp of water, then at sunset, she stops serenely to allow people to take a photo of her. Then she makes her way back, stopping off at a bar or two, to poke her head over the counter. It marks a passing of the day, a ritual, like the morning yoga class or the feeding of the cows on beach before the sun goes down. I asked if she had a name. "White Horse," they said.

I witnessed all of this from my Simrose beach hut and

got caught up in its rhythm. It seemed to form part of a constant thrum of activity, which was underpinned by the sound of the waves crashing on the shore. I arrived at 2am and couldn't believe how loud they were at high tide. I was woken by them several times during the course of my stay and had to wear earplugs. "Oh yeah – always get a hut further back from the beach," people said, who had been there before. The waves are the soundtrack to everything and even the yoga teacher used their rhythm to breathe against – a technique I learned called *ujjayi* or 'ocean breath'.

If I sound like I've gone all spiritual, I sort of have. People said, "Oh Goa isn't the real India", thinking of the trance scene the litter-strewn beaches of the north. Well it was real enough to me, and I loved it. I did yoga class every morning I could with Lucia, who was from Italy and filled with hypnotic phrases about the various chakra and how I could focus on them. I had had a stressful time at work before Christmas and was coming back to a promotion that promised an extremely busy time ahead so I made the most of the chance to connect with myself and the sea (which I love to be beside and float in a boat upon but I can't swim in).

The biggest surprise was finding that I knew most of the vinyasa poses already from my time training in contemporary dance. I didn't know that Martha Graham had nicked them all to become 'the mother of modern dance'. Even in the two weeks I was there I started to feel my old dance body coming back – strong back, strong core, a stretched feeling in my hips and legs – a feeling I never thought I would recreate.

I developed my own White Horse routine. It involved walking on the beach, yoga, then breakfast, reading on my hut deck, lunch, more reading, another walk, cocktails, dinner then drinks at a bar. As with my very first solo trip abroad, it took me three days to leave the resort. I was a little bit scared of what would be there (so much scaremongering about India, especially for women). But as it was Christmas, I just spent the first few days in the resort, enjoying the efforts the staff made to make it fun and festive. I spent Christmas Eve with a brother and sister from Manchester – the brother lives down the road from me in London. Small world...

On Boxing Day I decided I needed to venture out. I found a single strand of shops and stalls selling clothes, jewellery, spices, and copious sarongs. I found friendly shop-owning women, all telling me I was their 'first customer of the day' and therefore they were giving me 'the best deal'. Even though I knew it was all sales talk it was fun and I bought beach dresses and loose trousers. I didn't get hassled once by men other than to ask if I wanted a taxi. I felt safe. I spotted a bar on my way back with my spoils and liked its vibe, and promised myself I'd venture out later. It's always tough that first time. It always requires a bit of Dutch Courage to make that first step so I made mine a Caipirowska.

I pulled up a stool at Kopi Desa and immediately a guy from Birmingham slid into the seat next to me and asked if I'd mind chatting to him. As he rambled on, I could see a couple, obviously British, trying to catch my eye to see if I needed help. I can't remember how I made it over to them but I did and they said the guy had been hitting on lone women all day. It's always a British guy, never a local. They introduced the barman as 'the best-looking man in Goa'. I couldn't disagree.

Over the next few nights I met more Brits there, plus

Indians, Scandinavians and Coca-Cola the cow who popped in for a drink every evening. The bar is open to the street so you're surrounded by everything, from the bell-ringing bread boy on his bike in the early evening, to the beach dogs scouring for scraps. I spent New Year's Eve with friends I met in this bar, watching fireworks on the beach at H_2O. I had the best New Year's Day ever.

I'd started dating someone before Christmas and whilst I'd enjoyed the time we spent together I wasn't truly sure I was ready to commit to them. At first I thought my trip to Goa was getting in the way of progress, but in truth it gave me time to reflect and think about what I really wanted. I watched the White Horse, a symbol of freedom without restraint in many cultures, completing her daily ritual with no one to stop her. I remembered one of my favourite *Sex and the City* quotes, cited at the top of this post, and knew it applied to me. I thought about returning to Agonda, a place I already knew I loved, with a partner and I felt sad. I knew I wanted to come back on my own, with no one reining me in or saddling me with their needs and wants.

I knew I didn't want to be one of the many women with families I'd witnessed, anxious and hovering over their brood (and injured animals), unable to just relax by themselves and watch the ocean. I'd sat next to a woman on the plane out, who was separated by the aisle from her family and spent ten hours slightly angled towards them, watching them, whilst they completely ignored her and vegged out with dad. I didn't want to be a woman in an unhappy coupling, waiting until she's in a group to make sly digs at her partner. I've done that and it sucks.

I did want to be the free woman on New Year's Eve who whooped at fireworks with the happiest couple on earth, Lucy and Jason, who were on their honeymoon mega-trip. A couple who are happy to spend time with a single woman are rare indeed – and you know they are the strong ones who will last. And I did want to be the woman who shared a bottle of prosecco with the best-looking man in Goa when the fireworks were over.

If the New Year is about making choices and stepping forward with the right ones, then here I stand: unfettered, mane blowing in the breeze, stamping my hooves with joy.

CHEAT PLAY LIVE (EXTRACT)

PATONG BEACH, PHUKET, THAILAND, AUGUST 2010

I WATCHED the little plane on the map on the back of the seat fly its course over Europe, Asia and then South East Asia. I would be flying into Bangkok airport and then taking a linking flight to Phuket. Where I was going was somewhere 'real' travellers would probably avoid – Patong – but I needed a lovely hotel near a bustling town and that's what I got.

I revelled in everything that I take for granted now: the welcome drink of exotic fruit juice, the flowers decorating my bed and the towels sculpted into the shape of animals. It was August and the off-season, so they upgraded me to a beachfront room with a balcony overlooking the sea, framed by swaying palm trees. It was perfect. Or it would have been if I'd been on a romantic holiday for two.

One of the first things I did after I left my husband was book a holiday. I had never been anywhere outside the UK on my own but I suddenly felt the urge. I called a travel operator – how quaint! – and asked them where they could take me for a week or two for my budget. "Thailand," they said.

It was almost Bali, but crucially not Bali. I was very keen not to be an Eat Pray Love groupie. Thailand was where solo travellers went, knowing there would be other solo travellers. It was a well-worn path and that would give me a foundation to work from. I wanted somewhere that was far enough away that I wouldn't be tempted to fly back if I lost my nerve. A sixteen-hour flight would do it.

"I always wanted to go to Thailand," Graham said regretfully as soon as he discovered my plan. He offered to take me to the airport and I'll never forget the look on his face when he dropped me off. It said, "Wow, she's really doing this."

This time I didn't have to wait for him to finish three cigarettes before going through to departures, he wouldn't be making my cry at the other end for booking something he didn't like, or trying to photograph me in a microscopic bikini. This was a holiday for me and there would be no recourse to anyone else.

But oh, the despair. It kicked in on the first evening. I was in a paradise location, complete with Disney levels of butterflies dancing around the gardens between my room and the beach. I was surrounded by romantic couples and here I was on my own.

I drank cocktails at Happy Hour in a bid to cheer myself up, but I ended up crying into my Thai green curry in the restaurant. The staff didn't know what to do so they stayed away from me. I cried non-stop for three days and barely left my room. I cried for my failed marriage, the time I'd wasted with the wrong man, the time he'd wasted with the wrong woman, and the time I'd wasted with no men. I cried for what I'd done to Graham by cheating on him, because he didn't deserve it. I cried for the holiday adventures I'd had with him that I'd never have again, and I cried for the loss of coupledom. I didn't have my hand in anyone's hand and I was out there alone with no one caring.

But someone did care. Friends sent texts to see how I was getting on and I admitted that I felt miserable. I was getting up every morning to go to breakfast and wearing sunglasses because my eyes were so screwed up by all the crying. I pulled on a lovely dress to make myself feel better: a breakfast dress.

I've continued with this breakfast-dress tradition on holiday ever since. I often look more glamorous in the mornings than I do in the evenings. It's something I like to do for myself when I'm away and I recommend it. If I dress up at night, people think I'm 'on the lookout', so I dress up in the mornings instead. Breakfast dress.

One of my oldest friends from Hove days, Kay, texted with a few suggestions about what I might do to cheer myself up. There was a spa perched high up on a hill above the hotel that offered massages, manicures and pedicures and I resolved to have everything done.

I had never had beauty treatments until I'd had that Wicked Weasel wax done for Kenya. In my old life they seemed like a waste of time – who needed nice nails when you were on safari? But suddenly they were everything I needed.

With my cried-out piglet eyes I lay under towels and let a Thai woman walk all over my body. I let another woman paint my toe- and fingernails orchid pink and put matching flowers in my hair.

Afterwards, I went for a walk down to the bright white jetty that stuck out into the sea in front of the hotel. To get to it, I had to walk on a butterfly-filled path through the jungle. There were sunloungers on it with no one on them because it was the rainy season, and an ice-cream salesman downstairs. I decided to set up camp there.

I remember lying there and reading David Nicholls' novel One Day, in one day, marvelling that I had this glorious location all to myself. I forgot I was in crying mode and started to spend time just staring at the sea and my toenails. I found solace in a good old puzzle book I'd bought at the airport.

I texted Kay back: *"The pampering worked!"* She suggested I try a trip next – perhaps to see some elephants or a boat trip. I booked both.

I loved riding atop a naughty teenage elephant at a nearby sanctuary, where the animals were well-looked after. My animal thought it was fine to drop down into a few ditches on his way around the forest and I laughed each time he did. His mahout's conical hat bobbed in front of me as we swayed through the greenery and flitting butterflies.

I screamed with joy as the speedboat bashed against waves, hurtling towards Koh Phi Phi and James Bond Island. I got sunburned on the face and neck as I turned my head upwards towards the sun. I was coming back to life here, the wind blowing away the pain. I spent the day on and off the boat with a man my age and his young son. It was so nice to be part of a mini family for a day.

But I still hadn't gone into town on my own. I was too scared of what was outside the cocoon of the hotel. Kay looked it up for me: the town was only a tuktuk ride away.

That evening, I primed myself with Happy Hour cocktails and talked to a couple a bit older than me at the bar. I hoped that they hadn't see the piglet-eyed, wretched version of me – I wanted them to see a woman who was confident in the world in a nice dress, her nails done and flowers in her hair, all ready to hit the town. I bid them goodbye and went out to find a tuktuk.

There was a row of drivers lined up outside the hotel, all lounging in different positions around their vehicles.

"Patong?" I asked.

One nodded.

There I was, speeding towards the lights of town, a woman on her own. So adventurous! And so unnecessary: the tuktuk drive lasted less than three minutes. The town was well within walking distance and the tuktuks were there for frightened tourists like me. I laughed when I realised and so did the driver.

I hopped out of the tuktuk, heart beating fast, with the Dutch courage afforded by the two margaritas at the hotel bar. I was wearing a long purple maxi dress with a jewelled belt slung round my hips, boho-style. I looked down bustling Bangla Road filled with its souvenir shops, ping-pong bars, nightclubs and ladyboy dancers posing for photographs. It reminded me of parts of Brighton. Then I saw the bar for me – Murphy's. I knew I'd find a friendly face in an Irish pub.

I went in and pulled up a stool at the bar. There was a band on, covering Western rock songs with an impossibly beautiful Thai woman singing. In between songs, I turned to face the barman and blend into the bar. I was sure no one could see me up there, my back to the room, sipping on wine. No one approached and no one said anything, but I had found somewhere I could sit quietly and be part of the world outside the hotel.

On my second night, I knew what to do. I dressed down in shorts and a vest. I wanted to blend in more and not stand out in a long dress and a jewelled belt. I wanted to look like someone who backpacked all the time and rocked up at bars like this every day of her life, straight out of a Sheryl Crow song. There was no band on this time. Just me, facing the barman again, staying as still as I could so no one would notice me.

"Are you on your own?" an Aussie voice said.

I turned round to find a group of Aussies in their twenties bustling into the bar in brightly coloured singlets and board shorts.

"Kind of," I admitted, although I'd been doing a very good impression of being with two young women who were also sitting at the bar.

"Not any longer you're not. Come and join us!"

There were men and women in the group, all bright-eyed with their travels and good vibes. I'd seen tribes of them scooting around the island and envied their freedom. Especially the boys – it was clear that they could do anything they wanted whenever they wanted. I wanted their lives, but was that something a forty-three-year-old woman could ever have? I wasn't sure. But for now, sitting in an Irish bar with a group of Aussies for company was enough. A group of Aussies who suddenly parted in the middle to make way for their leader, Dougie.

Dougie had dark eyes and jet-black hair gelled up from his face into a Joey-from-Friends quiff. Dougie had the broad shoulders of a trainee Thai fighter. That's what he was doing there, he said.

After an hour of talking, he looked down at me with half-lidded eyes that showed me what he wanted. "Do you want to do a Phantom?" he asked.

"A Phantom?"

"Yeah – just get out of here without saying goodbye."

Ah my favourite – the French Exit – which I now know has a variety of different names around the world. I do it all the time – it takes away the need for lengthy goodbyes, and when people are drunk at the end of the night, they don't notice you've gone anyway.

We walked out, heads down, not saying a word to anyone. Dougie hailed a scooter taxi – the driver was a woman my age – and beckoned for me to get on behind him.

I clung on as we hurtled into the night. We stopped briefly at his hotel so he could collect a few things. The Thai woman turned to me and said, "I think he will be very good for you." She couldn't have been more right.

She dropped us at my hotel and we bumped into the couple I'd met at Happy Hour earlier. They were going to bed for an early night. I wasn't.

The next morning a pair of dark eyes and a shock of black hair peeped out from the white sheets as I made my way to the bathroom. "Where have you been all my life?" Dougie croaked, laughing.

I couldn't believe how good-looking Dougie was, and that he was in my bed. I couldn't believe that he was twenty-four. But for some reason I wanted him out of my room quickly, so that I could get my breakfast dress on and start my routine. Why I didn't keep him in my bed all day I'll never know.

I went on another boat trip and met two Aussie men closer to my age. They seemed friendly and happy to hang out with me. It was only later that I discovered that one of them had designs on me for that night – the other guy told me he'd agreed to back off and leave me to his friend. But I wasn't interested in either of them, beyond companionship in a foreign town.

We went to Murphy's Bar that evening. The guy who'd agreed to 'back off' made noises about leaving and I said I might go too. That didn't go down too well with the other guy's plan and he started to get aggressive. He clearly thought I owed him sex as he'd deigned to spend the whole day with me being a 'nice guy'. Where was his reward?

I surreptitiously texted Dougie under the table and told him I needed rescuing. He was in a bar down the road. Within minutes he appeared in Murphy's with his friends and walked over to where we were sitting. He started talking to the guy as though he'd known him for years whilst simultaneously making it clear that he wanted him gone. No sooner had he been ushered out of the pub than Dougie was back by my side.

Bo Phut Beach, Koh Samui, Thailand, December 2010

I was wearing a red Wicked Weasel bikini and sitting in the corner of the pool, looking out over the bay. I had a view over the town– it had its fair share of tourists, but it was less 'Brighton' than Patong. It had boutique dress shops, French cafés and a picturesque broken jetty which, if Instagram hadn't only just been invented, would've been a huge selling point, especially with Thai children playing all over it.

It turned out the eight days I'd spent in Phuket in August were just a rehearsal. I'd spent three of them crying in my room and the last five had shown me what could be on the menu. As soon as I got home, I booked a second holiday, this time over Christmas for two weeks, to Koh Samui. I booked a room in a guest house with a rooftop pool by the sea in Fisherman's Village, Bo Phut, in the north of the island.

I spent my first few days shopping for new breakfast dresses and trying out the local cafés and restaurants, which all seemed to be French. I booked a few trips and went to bars alone in the evenings. Bo Phut beach itself wasn't that great for sunbathing or walking so I took taxis to Chaweng beach down the coast. It was a huge strand of golden sand filled with bars and sunloungers.

But the holiday wasn't quite the sparkling new experience I'd had in Phuket. I tried too hard to attract another Dougie and it backfired. I went on a boat trip on New Year's Eve and spent most of it with two young French men. I wore my red Wicked Weasel bikini under my shorts and lay out on the beaches we stopped at, hoping the bikini would lure them in. But they weren't interested. Another guy I'd met in a bar dropped me for a Thai woman he'd hired.

I planned to spend New Year's Eve on Bo Phut beach watching the fireworks, but it started to rain and I was alone. I felt very sorry for myself. I stayed in my room and cried.

Salvation came in the form of two Thai women. I had met them that day in the beauty salon where I went for my now-customary manicures, pedicures and massages. They were called Su and Bo – Su was my age and Bo was in her twenties.

Su-Bo shyly asked me if I would like to go out with them on New Year's Day. They would show me some places where Thai people liked to go and '*farang*' (foreigners) didn't.

What I didn't realise until 1pm the next day is that Su-Bo would turn up on one small motorbike and expect me to sit in between them. I joked that we made a *farang* sandwich and they laughed.

We buzzed around the island nodding and smiling to

the families piled four or five high onto tiny bikes. We had a puncture and visited a Thai garage to get it fixed. Even that was fun.

Su-Bo took me for lunch at a beauty spot that had famous penis- and vagina-shaped rock formations – Hin Ta (grandfather) and Hin Yai (grandmother) rocks. They giggled when I pointed at the white surf crashing around the base of Hin Yai. We posed for selfies together at a time before selfies. I look large and white in the pictures – the Thai women are tiny and tanned.

On the bike ride home to Bo Phut, my hair blew back as we faced the golden rays of the sunset. I couldn't help grinning. I knew I should have been wearing a helmet but I thought to myself, if I die now, it will be ok, because I have had this moment.

We met again later that evening to go clubbing. The New Year's Eve revellers were still going from the previous evening and we joined them at the Green Mango club in Chaweng. Su-Bo could only get in because they were with me and they stuck to me closely as the security guards checked us out. They told me that Thai women were banned from the club unless they were with *farang* friends. They didn't want customers being hustled for business by women who were selling themselves.

I bought buckets of cocktails for the three of us and we started dancing. I found myself up on stage with Bo after Su left us early to go back to her family. I was dancing with Andrew – a tall, dark, young Australian who was still high from the previous night. He couldn't believe I was forty-three. I couldn't believe I was either.

This was the holiday I should have had at twenty-three.

CHEAT PLAY LIVE

ONE WOMAN'S JOURNEY TO FEARLESSNESS AND FREEDOM

Moving and deeply emotional
HELLO! magazine

Raw, truthful and brave. I couldn't put it down
Carol Drinkwater, actor, film maker, author of *The Olive Farm*

ON A BEACH in California in 2008, Lisa finds a shell on a rock, its two halves open to the sky. On the outside it is sea-worn and unremarkable, but on the inside it gleams like a jewel. It is as though it is lying there, waiting to be found and cherished – like her. She uses the picture she takes of that shell to set up an online profile that will end her marriage. It leads her to more beaches around the world – to Kenya, Thailand, Turkey, Egypt and India – in search of freedom from the fear of a life alone, from society's expectations of a fortysomething woman, and the freedom to choose how she wants to live.

For fans of *Eat Pray* Love by Elizabeth Gilbert and *Wild* by Cheryl Strayed, Lisa Edwards' story is about the search for a life beyond the one prescribed for women: marriage, babies and a high-flying career. Childfree by choice, she is determined to travel solo, going on holidays on her own, as well as to restaurants, bars and even clubs. But grieving for her parents, she begins to depend on the anaesthetic that alcohol gives her and it steers her life in unexpected ways. During the course of her journey she dates married men, younger men, men her own age and Muslim men, but none of them are prepared to give her her freedom. In India, she discovers yoga and a tribe of women who show her a new path, breaking the lock on the secret she's been keeping inside her since she was a little girl.

- *Cheat Play Live* by Lisa Edwards is out now (Redwood Tree Publishing, £4.99 (ebook), £6.99 (paperback)

ACKNOWLEDGMENTS

I'd like to thank all the women I've met who've shown me another way to live and who've formed an invisible chain of support as I rode the solo rollercoaster.

To Angela Elkins, who first opened my eyes to the way we are programmed to think coupledom is the only valid life choice.

To all the sparkling hiking ladies who leave unadventurous men on their sofas while they get out and explore the world. I salute you.

To Iris, whom I met as I was putting this book together. You are the person I'm writing for and you will never look back.

To Shubham, who is my boyfriend, yet not my boyfriend, who is running alongside his White Horse, not trying to tame her or tether her. May we run together always, wild and free.

ABOUT THE AUTHOR

Lisa Edwards is a former publisher who is now a freelance writer, editor, agent and yoga teacher. She grew up in North Wales, but has lived mostly in southeast England. She lives in Worthing, West Sussex, where she lives alone and walks by the sea every day. She splits her time between the UK and India.

amazon.com/author/lisa_edwards

facebook.com/becauseyoucan50

twitter.com/Redwoods1

instagram.com/redwoods1

linkedin.com/in/lisa-edwards-34991115

goodreads.com/lisaedwards

ALSO BY LISA EDWARDS

Because You Can is the ongoing story of a woman who left her marriage in 2010 and is actively exploring the world and writing her about her experiences. Read all of Lisa's blog posts on her Wordpress site, join her Facebook page and sign up to her newsletter for news of her latest books:

All the links you need: https://linktr.ee/redwoods1

No drink tastes as good as sober feels…

In January 2019, I stopped drinking and I couldn't believe that I'd been in the grip of a highly addictive drug for so long. I didn't know it was extremely harmful to my physical and mental health, and I didn't know I was an addict. Read about my experience, as a fiftysomething woman with two decades of addiction behind her, finally kicking the habit and leading her life with a clear mind.

Includes:

- my twelve-step guide to becoming sober and maintaining it
- my sober diary
- an extract from my memoir, *Cheat Play Live*, where my sober journey is explored in detail

Printed in Dunstable, United Kingdom

73971036R00069